Smallmouth Bass Fly Fishing

A Practical Guide

Smallmouth Bass Fly Fishing

A Practical Guide

by Terry and Roxanne Wilson
Illustrated by Lefty Wilson

ISBN 978-1-58597-431-3
Library of Congress Control Number: 2007924859

LEATHERS
PUBLISHING

4500 College Boulevard
Overland Park, Kansas 66211
888-888-7696
www.leatherspublishing.com

DEDICATION

To those whose efforts restore or preserve clean water, free-flowing streams, and smallmouth bass habitat.

Authors' Biography

TERRY AND ROXANNE WILSON

The Wilsons have presented innovative, practical fly-fishing methods for bass, bluegill, crappie, gar, and channel catfish for more than twenty years in over a hundred magazine articles published in *Fly-fishing and Tying Journal, The Flyfisher, Midwest Fly-fishing, Warmwater Fly-fishing, Fly-fishing Quarterly, Bassmaster, Ontario Out of Doors,* and many others. They are staff writers for St. Louis-based *Outdoor Guide Magazine.* Terry's original flies for bluegills, largemouth bass, and smallmouth bass have been featured in *Fly Fish America* and *Fly-fishing and Tying Journal* and have been included in the books *Innovative Flies and Techniques* published in 2005 and *Federation of Fly-fishers Fly Pattern Encyclopedia* published in 2000. Roxanne's photos appear in their magazine articles, books, and slide shows.

Their first book, *Bluegill Fly-fishing and Flies*, was published by Frank Amato Publications, Inc. in April, 1999. *Largemouth Bass*

Fly-fishing: Beyond the Basics, their second book, was published in 2001. *Smallmouth Bass Fly-fishing: A Practical Guide* is their third book.

Terry and Roxanne are members of the Missouri Smallmouth Alliance and are active life members of the Federation of Fly-fishers. They were presented with the Federation's Don Harger Memorial Award in 1996 for their contributions to the sport of fly-fishing. Roxanne was named 1994 Woman of the

Year by the Federation's Southern Council. They are members of the Federation's Warmwater Conservation Committee.

The Wilsons live in southwest Missouri, where they enjoy fishing the streams and lakes of the Ozark Mountains.

ACKNOWLEDGEMENTS

Nearly fifty years of our pursuit of smallmouth bass with fly rods have enabled them to teach us about their habits, preferences, needs, and lifestyles, but a lot of our knowledge has been gleaned from the many folks with whom we've had the pleasure of sharing the sport. Guides from the Canadian Shield to the southernmost portion of the bronzeback's range; fly shop owners, their employees and clientele; fly tyers and rod builders; conservation officers; fisheries biologists; as well as those we've been privileged to share the special places smallmouths live have all contributed to these pages. We are indebted to each, even those whose names were forgotten long before this project was contemplated.

These are the generous folks whose help and advice facilitated writing this book. Thank you for helping make our efforts a labor of love:

John "Lefty" Wilson, whose illustrations enhance our words, for sharing the joy of guiding in the Boundary Waters Canoe Area and our love of fly-fishing for smallmouth bass.

Dave Whitlock, whose generosity with his wealth of knowledge, innovative fly patterns, and time is deeply appreciated.

Dave Duffy for sharing his fly patterns and beautiful North Carolina waters.

Rob Woodruff for his fly patterns and for introducing us to the waters of southeast Oklahoma.

Duane Hada for his fly recipes and for guiding us on his North Arkansas rivers and spring creeks.

Miles and Michelle Riley of Riley's Station Resort, hosts who graciously shared their knowledge of Arkansas' famous Buffalo River.

Ethan Wright for an exciting ride through the spectacular Kiamichi Mountains to amazing smallmouth fishing, and to Jesse King of Three Rivers Fly Shop for sharing southeast Oklahoma's unique waters with us.

Butch McElwain, the late Hank Reifuss, and Tom Wilson for introducing us to their tactics on dissimilar, but exceptional smallmouth waters.

Harvey Ragsdale for offering his talents and time in assisting us with preparing the flies in this book for photography.

Mark Stephens, an extraordinary photographer, for his expertise in presenting our collection of smallmouth flies.

Tom and Neal Conry of Peregrine Productions in Ainsworth, Iowa, whose professional graphic abilities have been invaluable and for sharing their home rivers.

John Henry, fly tyer and fishing companion extraordinaire, for sharing his smallmouth haunts and time on the water.

The many creative tyers who have shared their original patterns, tying advice, and knowledge of smallmouth bass.

The state chapters of The Smallmouth Alliance for their efforts in preserving and improving smallmouth bass waters.

Special thanks to the Federation of Fly-fishers for providing a forum for discussion of smallmouth conservation and their ongoing support of the preservation of native fish in their native waters.

CONTENTS

INTRODUCTION

One of the first fishing guides we ever hired back in the 1960's was for the purpose of pursuing smallmouth bass. We had pulled into a tiny North Arkansas hamlet's gas station that doubled as headquarters for a guide service. A round-faced balding man sat at the business entrance in a wooden chair with its back legs sawed short so its occupant could rest in a semi-reclining position. He was a self-proclaimed "go gitter." His appearance suggested otherwise until he explained that at 7:30 each morning he'd drive his wife to work and at 4:30 each evening he'd "go git 'er." We fell for his old joke hook, line, and split shot. Between his arduous assignments he was free to share his "lifetime of fish'n secrets" from a 20-foot jon boat with anyone willing to part with his guiding fee and bring along the fried chicken.

Shortly before eight the next morning, we were clattering down a dusty pothole-infested path toward "the crick" in an ancient pickup truck that threatened to rattle apart with each bone-jarring bump. We unloaded the boat on a shaded gravel bar below a concrete slab ford and rigged up. Our guide was aghast to discover that we had brought "fly poles" and adamantly declared them unusable due to the lack of backcasting room on his "crick." But, despite his reservations, we were able to present an assortment of streamers and poppers effectively enough to land and release nearly eighty smallmouths between 10 and 17 inches. It was this trip, more than all the previous ones, that launched our love affair with bronzebacks. The stream was Arkansas' famous Crooked Creek, at that time one of the nation's greatest smallmouth waters.

Since that magical day so long ago we've continually sought to renew our acquaintance with these admirable fighters. We've come to adore fly-fishing for smallmouth bass for all the standard reasons. They are subtly handsome, superb fighters that frequently leap when hooked, pull strongly, and have the staying power of Olympic athletes. Moreover, smallmouths are often found in places of spectacular beauty.

The sport of fly-fishing for smallmouth bass has a history that is uniquely North American. Long ago, they were zealously pursued with cane fly rods on the James and the White Rivers of Missouri and Arkansas, where fly-fishers cast from twenty-foot long boats made from three pine boards. Cork poppers fashioned from wine bottle stoppers adorned with wild turkey tail feathers and neck feathers from fighting cocks served as homemade flies in the early twentieth century. The union of cane rods, imitation bugs, and smallmouth bass allow each of us to feel an instant kinship with James Henshall and all of the nameless practitioners of this exhilarating sport.

We have written this book for those who would share our love of catching smallmouth bass from beautiful streams, bountiful reservoirs, and cold northern lakes. Its pages are filled with the produce of our experiences, hours of research, and the input from countless discussions with fellow fly-fishers we encountered along the way.

CHAPTER 1
THE FIGHTINGEST FISH

It's difficult to visualize the typical smallmouth bass fly-fisher. The confusion stems from recognition of the many tactics that were borrowed from trout and large-mouth bass anglers. Wading streams, drag-free drifts, and matching hatches are associated with trout while locator-equipped bass boats, sinking lines, and structure orientation belong in the realm of the largemouth bass. Engaging small-mouth bass might involve delicately casting a size-16 nymph into a riffle or lobbing a 1/0 deer-hair bug toward a rock-strewn mid-lake hump.

The confusion ends with the hook-set. Smallmouth bass often battle near the water's surface — and frequently, above it. Fly-fishing for them is a highly visual game. Smallmouth are sleek, well-muscled athletes with speed, power, and stamina. Smallmouth bass, sometimes called brown bass, bronze-backs, Oswego bass, redeye bass, but scientifically known as *Microperus dolomieui*, are gorgeously packaged bronze bomb-shells that feed aggressively, yet selectively, on prey easily rep-licated at the tying vise. Nineteenth-century author James A.

Henshall, in his famous work *Book of the Black Bass,* called them " . . . inch for inch and pound for pound the gamest fish that swims." Although Dr. Henshall did not specify which of the black basses he designated for the honor we agree with generations of anglers that smallmouth bass are warmwater's fightingest fish.

The bass of Terry's youth were largemouths found in the few farm ponds and a city lake within bicycling distance. Smallmouth bass existed only in the tattered pages of barbershop magazines that told of exotic waters located in far away places. Toward the end of his twelfth summer, and his first as a fly-fisher, a six-hour journey took the family to an aunt and uncle and a house full of cousins. Uncle Albert, an outdoorsman of enviable skill who was regarded by family and friends as a fishing guru, promised to lead an expedition to his favorite local river in pursuit of bass. Armed with hardware store cork poppers, Terry cast behind the branches of a deadfall identified by his mentor as productive water. Instantly, the fly disappeared from the surface. A 15-inch bottle rocket shot skyward, then executed a series of somersaults that led to an overrun spool and a wild chase scene across a gravel bar to keep from snapping the tippet. Amid shouted advice from an entourage of cousins, the fish continued to dive and leap across the pool until loose coils of line could be retrieved. Finally, the prize was captured and admired in a huddle of preteen exuberance. Two things were abundantly clear: Uncle Albert's bass were much different than Terry's and they were a lot angrier about being hooked.

Physical Characteristics

A smallmouth's upper jaw does not extend beyond its eye and itsdorsal fin has a very shallow notch in contrast to a largemouth bass's. Coloration of an adult smallmouth bass varies widely and is most affected by its physical environment. Smallmouths from shaded, nutrient-rich water have dark brown backs with a bronze

When fly-fishing for small mouth bass is involved, it's love at first strike.

cast and dark olive vertical bars on their sides, while spring creek bass found in full sunlight over light-colored bottoms are sometimes pale tan with light brown bars. In the same pool it's possible to catch both light- and dark-colored fish depending on the bottom's content and color as well as the angle of sunlight penetration. On a recent float trip we slowly drifted past 14- to 16-inch smallmouths cruising over a mid-stream light-colored bottom. We landed two that were colored a very pale, mottled tan. Within the same pool we caught another smallmouth that was coaxed from an undercut bank. That fish was a rich brown/olive in color with the smallmouth's signature iridescent bronze sheen. These fish looked very different from one another, yet they were probably from the same gene pool and perhaps the same year class. Their chameleon-like ability to change colors is nature's way of allowing smallmouths to conceal themselves from their prey and their predators.

The world record smallmouth came from Dale Hollow Reservoir on the Kentucky-Tennessee border. It weighed in at 11 pounds 15 ounces and was caught in 1955. Mid-South reservoirs like Dale Hollow and Alabama's Wheeler Lake produce smallmouths up to 8 pounds each season and figure to be the sites of future record fish. It should be noted that a 5-pound smallmouth is an exceptional catch whereas a 5-pound largemouth is relatively common.

The lifestyle of smallmouths in moving water is much more arduous and consequently the size of the fish, particularly in regard to weight, can be substantially less than those found in lakes. Even in blue ribbon streams like the Androscoggin in Maine, Virginia's James River, and the St. Croix in Wisconsin, a smallmouth of 4 pounds is outstanding. Usually, river fish are 12 to 15 inches in length and, especially when aided by current, their fights are memorable.

Growth rates in either still or moving waters depend on the amount of food available and its caloric value, as well as the temperature of the water and the length of the growing season. In an infertile stream, for example, it may take 4 years for a bass to reach 9 inches in length while large, fertile lakes can grow a 9-incher by the end of the second summer. Even under ideal conditions 7 to 10 years are required to grow a smallmouth of 18 inches.

The Life Cycle of Smallmouth Bass

Growth rates and latitude cause smallmouth bass to become sexually mature at different ages. In northern climates males reach maturity at 3 years of age when they reach about 9 inches in length. In the mid-South, smallmouths usually mature at 2 years.

When water temperatures reach between 60 and 70 degrees, sexually mature males move into the shallows to prepare their nests. This occurs in early April through May or, in the northern portion of its range, into mid-June. Often, they migrate to suitable spawning sites in the smaller tributaries or rivers that feed large reservoirs. It's believed that in stillwater male smallmouth bass return to the same nesting sites every year, generation after generation. Males use their tails to fan out gravel and sand on the bottom and may even carry some of the debris out of their 14- to 30-inch depressions by using their mouths. Depending upon the clarity of the water and the suitability of the bottom content the nests can be built in depths less than 2 feet or as deep as 22 feet. If the water is turbid, the nests will be relatively shallow while very clear water will force the nest building deeper. When the nest is completed the male selects a ripe female and drives her to his nest. Females produce from 2,000 to 7,000 eggs per pound of body weight but they commonly deposit as few as several hundred to 2,000 in a single nest. When the male fertilizes the eggs, the female is driven from the area and is commonly selected by several other males to contribute to their nests. Normally a male will fertilize the eggs of three females but it may fertilize as few as one. The average nest contains about 2,000 eggs but it can hold as many as 10,000. If, for some reason, the males are removed from their nests at this point, no other males will assume guard duty and the nests will be vulnerable to predation and silt might cover the eggs, thus reducing the oxygen necessary for the eggs to survive. Depending on water temperature, the eggs incubate in 2 to 9 days. Fry are completely black except for the gold irises of their eyes and leave the nest within a few hours to fend for themselves. Smallmouth bass provide little parental care, but males usually defend the brood vigorously for a short period. If the nesting success is erased by plummeting temperatures or high water the process may be repeated and might extend into July. A succession of bad conditions can cause the females to drop their eggs without fertilization and the year's spawn is aborted.

Life for smallmouth bass fry is tenuous at best. Only about one in every thousand hatchlings survives until fall when the hardships increase. The fry's first food is minute organisms, but after a few weeks it feeds on insect larvae. When fry are an inch long, they feed on small fish until they grow large enough to devour the crayfish that will become one of their dietary staples.

Smallmouth growth rates are highly variable, but even under optimum conditions they're not fast growers. Survival for many years is necessary for a fish to grow to sporting size and a trophy fish of 20 inches or more must have excellent health and an abundant diet for at least 10 years. Those who catch and keep smallmouth bass are not only removing fish that have beaten the odds to attain their size but they might also remove from the gene pool smallmouths with the characteristics that make the achievement possible.

The Kiamichi Mountain streams in southeastern Oklahoma are part of the small-mouth's original range.

Smallmouth Distribution

Seventeenth century French trappers caught smallmouth bass along the St. Lawrence River. Smallmouths claimed an original range that included the lakes and rivers of the St. Lawrence area, the Great Lakes, upper Mississippi, Ohio, and Tennessee drainage systems west to Minnesota, south to northern Alabama, and west to the Kiamichi Mountains of southeastern Oklahoma.

As transplants, smallmouth bass have done well in some areas such as Maine and Canadian lakes while they have struggled to gain footholds in many other regions. The reason probably relates most to competition for food and living, spawning, and rearing areas. Smallmouth bass aren't purely a cool water or a warmwater species. They have to compete with largemouths, northern pike, walleyes, brown and rainbow trout, salmon, and muskie as well as panfish, so while they are widely distributed today, there are many areas in which they are not the dominant species. Optimum conditions include suitable habitat and freedom from major competition. These combined conditions are rare outside their original range. The result is that a specific area of a lake or stream that does support these conditions harbors a high percentage of the smallmouth population while most of the particular body of water might be devoid of them altogether.

The smallmouth bass began its travels on America's railroads. Some crossed mountain ranges in the tender buckets that were used to dip water from rail-side lakes and rivers. These accidental stockings scattered smallmouths to diverse watersheds. As long as the watersheds where these stockings took place had clean water and rocky areas, the adaptable smallmouth claimed a niche in the ecosystem.

Early intentional stocking efforts were very primitive. Smallmouths were frequently hauled in milk cans from one location to another. It would be hard to imagine that mortality rates were anything but extremely high. Still, it was a method that was eventually successful. The survivors that were able to adapt to their new environment passed on the characteristic of hardiness to generations of their offspring. The earliest stockings were close to rail lines. In the 1920's rail cars in Ontario, Canada were specially equipped to transport smallmouth bass. Eventually, in some rugged areas pack trains consisting of sure-footed mules were used to carry fingerlings to remote locations. The result is that today anglers can enjoy the thrill of smallmouth bass in 47 states and all of Europe. Most of the European smallmouth stockings took place in the latter part of the nineteenth century. France received the earliest in 1869 from the United States. Several African nations also have stocked smallmouth bass. These plantings took place between 1937 and 1949.

At present, only Florida, Louisiana, and Alaska do not list state records for smallmouth bass. According to the National Fresh Water Fishing Hall of Fame the state records in 45 of 47 states exceed 5 pounds. Nineteen states boast a smallmouth in excess of 8 pounds, but four additional states are within 2 ounces of the mark. Only Tennessee, North Carolina, and Alabama can claim fish of 10 pounds or more as their records. Nearly 90 percent of the record smallmouths were taken from stillwater and the rest were caught from large rivers. The Fishing Hall of Fame also has a category for fly-fishers that's based on tippet strength. The largest fly rod-caught smallmouth listed is an 8 pound 12 ounce giant taken in 1966 from the Columbia River in the state of Washington. That fish is also the state record smallmouth there. Most encouraging of all is the Hall of Fame category, "Fly-fishing Catch & Release."

The long-term success of stocking smallmouth bass, both intentionally and accidentally, have truly made the species an all-American gamefish. The fact that enough fingerlings from milk-can stockings in the 1920's survived to spread the species to new watersheds doesn't mean that stocking is wise. The additions to the gene pool might weaken the strain that already exists there. It is, therefore, even more necessary that smallmouth aficionados are relentless in their conservation efforts and vigilant against any threat to the species or its environment. It's critically important that anglers come to respect smallmouth bass as the favored gamefish they are.

Homebody or Wanderer?

Despite its well-known reputation as a homebody, it's difficult to generalize about smallmouth bass movements. For any water to support a stable population, fish must be able to locate the things that meet their needs. They must have suitable spawning and rearing sites, adequate food supplies, and water quality and temperatures within their tolerance range. Sometimes it's necessary, despite their genetic inclination, that they move considerable distances to meet these needs. Competition from other species may influence this movement. If the best feeding and holding areas are occupied by a large population of competing species, for example, the smallmouth may be forced to become the marginal species. It's primarily the waters where this inter-species competition is not a major factor that non-native smallmouths have become dominant.

The most obvious and observable migrations take place in streams when rising temperatures and rising waters promote movements to locate suitable spawning sites. Most of the time the movements are upstream, but there are, according to scientific research, exceptions when smallmouths inexplicably move downstream. Whether this movement occurs because of instinctive urges to return to the places they were born or simply because riffles are more easily negotiated during periods of high water that coincide with rising temperatures is anybody's guess.

Many believe that stream smallmouths live out their lives within the same one-mile stretch of stream, but recent research indicates that may be the exception rather than the rule. U. S. Fish and Wildlife Service biologist Craig Springer reports that research by John Lyons and Paul Kanehl of the Wisconsin Department of Natural Resources tells a very different story.

According to their study, "The average total movement of all fish was just over four miles. All fish but one moved in an upstream direction, the loner moved downstream a total of seven miles."

Summertime smallmouths tended to be much more confined to home areas where food was abundant and their comfort needs regarding water temperature, well-oxygenated water, and protective cover was available. The adult smallmouths tracked in the same study, " . . . stayed in a comparatively small, confined area, staying in a home area of less than 700 feet long." Floods triggered movement outside this area in the summer. While this observation was more consistent with accepted smallmouth behavior, the studied Wisconsin fish changed their behavior in mid-August and began to wander. Their movements were random. Some moved upstream, some in both directions "as much as eleven miles." Their wanderlust appeared to last about 2 months before the fish settled into their winter homes around mid-November.

According to Springer, "What smallmouths did over winter is perhaps the most revealing finding in the study." Anglers as well as fisheries biologists have long believed that as the water temperatures drop, smallmouths become increasingly lethargic, eventually not feeding at all while occupying the deepest portions of pools. But the smallmouths in the Wisconsin study "remained active all winter long, even in water just above freezing. They took up housekeeping in an area over the length of a football field and keyed to slow-moving, rocky runs sometimes less than 3 feet deep, even when 10-foot-deep pools were nearby." Another alternative for some smallmouths is the comfort and feeding opportunities that exist in the comparative warmth of large spring holes and spring-fed tributaries. These springs generally stay in the mid- to upper fifty-degree range throughout the winter. We regularly fish one such spring branch and catch many smallmouths while snow blankets the streambanks and ice forms in our guides.

Is the Lyons-Kanehl study the last word in stream smallmouth movement through the seasons? Of course not. The study is based on a small sampling of fish in a restricted area. More research is necessary before even generalized conclusions can be drawn, but this study does seem to shoot holes in the previously accepted theories of smallmouth movements. As Springer relates, "according to Lyons, their research raised a lot more questions than it brought answers." It's reasonable to postulate that just as their human counterparts don't all respond to the same stimuli in the same way, neither do all smallmouths behave alike. Some may move long distances in spring and fall while others carve out a niche that satisfies their needs in a relatively short span of river. Some may actually conform to the preconceived notion that smallmouths are homebodies while others within the same population may be inveterate wanderers.

The movements of smallmouth bass in still water may be equally diverse. Smallmouths tend to be based in distinct areas of larger lakes. Again, changing conditions and the presence of competing species may force unpredictable movement. There is, for example, evidence that Great Lakes smallmouths follow forage in open water in summer and fall to the exclusion of other prey. These radical movements may not be associated with the lifestyle preference of the fish so much as the necessity of filling its needs. It may simply be that smallmouths feed on what is most easily available to them. Large, fertile waters offer the bass the opportunity to be selective. They might follow huge schools of baitfish and feed opportunistically. These bass have chosen a very active lifestyle whereas another population of smallmouths in the same massive fertile lake might forage along rocky outcroppings for crayfish. The smallmouth population in a smaller or less fertile lake really doesn't have many available options. In relatively small waters, the smallmouth's lifestyle is more sedentary and it is more likely to focus upon crayfish populations.

Proponents of fishing tournaments contend that tagging studies of smallmouth bass released at bass tournament weigh-in stations located miles from the places where the fish were caught showed that most bass quickly find their way back to their home areas, but the scientific studies we consulted supported much different conclusions. A study of derby-caught smallmouth bass in Grand River, Ontario by Christopher M. Bunt and David P. Philipp of the Illinois Natural History Survey and Steven J. Cooke of the Department of Natural Resources and Environmental Science of the University of Illinois was conducted between 1995 and 1999. The fishing tournament is an annual catch-and-release event and all fish caught throughout the river are brought to a centrally located weigh-in station, held for a few hours, then trucked to points along the river before they were returned to the water. Eighty percent of the radio-tagged released bass remained in the immediate vicinity for a month or more while the remaining twenty percent traveled many miles to return to their capture site. Gene R. Wilde, an associate professor in the Wildlife and Fisheries Management Institute at Texas Tech University "compiled published and unpublished estimates of dispersal distances by black basses (*Micropterus spp.*) captured and released alive in fishing tournaments." Results showed that only 32% of smallmouths returned to the capture site. Another "26% of smallmouth bass dispersed less than 1.6 km from their release sites." Wilde also concluded that there "was no difference in dispersal differences for fish captured and released in rivers versus those released in lakes and reservoirs." While we suspect lake smallmouths are more mobile than river fish, once again, the obvious conclusion must be that more scientific studies are necessary to understand the movements of smallmouth bass in different seasons, circumstances, and diverse locations.

Needs and Preferences

To flourish, smallmouths need relatively clean water that warms to no less than sixty degrees in the summertime. Stream smallmouths prefer a good percentage of riffles, a moderate flow, and bottom content that has gravel, chunk rock, boulders, and/or bedrock. Lake inhabitants prefer clear, rocky locations with a minimum depth of around 25 feet. Smallmouth bass that inhabit both areas need spawning sites, rearing pools, and abundant food sources ranging from insect larva to sustain the fry to minnows and crayfish for larger specimens.

Even with requirements that seem relatively diverse, smallmouths are fussy about where they live. Some reservoirs that do not harbor smallmouth populations have streams that bring water into them and streams below their dams with good numbers of smallmouths. However, the reservoirs themselves have none or very few smallmouth bass despite appearing to meet all the species' requirements. Other similar reservoirs nearby with feeder streams and outlet creeks can host vibrant populations.

We've caught smallmouths from dingy water that appeared to lack enough oxygen for their survival and from sections of streams that had mud banks and little rock. We've also caught them in water that was just above freezing and, in southeast Oklahoma, in water over 90 degrees. It would seem that while smallmouths are very intolerant of some conditions in their environment, they are overall a highly adaptable species. We know of one population that escaped a state park lake stocking and took up residence in the stream below the dam. The conservation department abandoned the lake's stocking program, but 45 years later offspring of the river fugitives still occupy a rocky area at the base of a bridge abutment in a muddy little stream that drains agricultural cropland. We never heard a report of anyone encountering them elsewhere in that creek. This tenacious willingness to cling to whatever is available is obviously the same characteristic that enabled the species to survive primitive stocking conditions that expanded their range throughout North America and across Europe. But it's also the same quality that causes the fish to be the dominant species in so few situations. Across most of its range the smallmouth is a secondary or even marginal species. So while it may be difficult to determine exactly which combination of circumstances is necessary to sustain a population, it is not at all difficult to determine where, in a given body of water, they will take up residence. The portion of the lake or stream that has the most preferred qualities may well host nearly 100 percent of that watershed's smallmouth population. One of our home lakes supports a secondary population that occupies only 10 percent of the lake's structure according to the Department of Conservation, yet the bass are thriving and have produced Missouri's record smallmouth bass. Despite clean water, rocky shorelines, and huge forage base the competition from other species appears to limit its range and numbers. Competing species in this particular lake include largemouth bass, walleye, crappie, white bass, and sunfish. It seems reasonable that their range and home territory may overlap enough to keep the smallmouths confined.

Our observation is that the occurrence of chunk rock is the most easily identifiable component that attracts and holds smallmouth bass. While we have fished populations that seemed to relate to uneven cracks of bottom bedrock and others that clung to the only available gravel along an otherwise silted bottom, the water where smallmouths are most at home has rock of dissimilar sizes. If a given piece of water, either still or moving, has lots of rock and a secondary smallmouth population, the smallmouth bass will take up residence in areas where gravel- to basketball- to Volkswagen-sized rock is most abundant. Even in waters where smallmouths are the primary species they don't tend to spread out over the water randomly but instead congregate in areas of the most diverse rock size.

The Menu

Tiny smallmouth hatchlings begin their lives feeding on microscopic organisms but soon add tiny fish to their diets. As they continue to grow they learn to feed opportunistically and their diets expand to terrestrial insects, larger nymphs, emergent insects, and eventually crustaceans. Crayfish are so associated with smallmouth bass that many anglers believe the species has a taste preference for them. Indeed, if smallmouth can locate where crayfish are abundant the crustaceans will comprise up to 80 percent of their diet. But it's likely that taste has nothing to do with the circumstance. Availability and ease of capture causes smallmouths to focus on crayfish as the main course on their menu. Crayfish are easy to capture because they are poor swimmers. They can only thrust themselves backward and flap their tails to propel themselves a foot or two at a time. They use current to assist their escapes where possible, but they're no match for gamefish. Smallmouths whose environments include lots of crayfish live relatively sedentary lifestyles.

Despite an abundance of crayfish, some populations of smallmouths, particularly those in large lakes and reservoirs, spend most of the summer feeding on minnows. The caloric intake from fish is much higher than crayfish meals of equal size, but the expenditure of energy in chasing and capturing baitfishes is high as well. Although research into the growth rates of both crayfish-focused and minnow-focused smallmouth populations is lacking, the observations of fishermen reveal no discernable difference. The evidence is that the baitfish-feeding smallmouths switched from one species of minnow to another from time to time. Their reasons for this may have been chance encounter or may actually have coincided with the prey that was most available. In mid-South reservoirs it's common for smallmouths to travel in close proximity to huge schools of baitfish and attack them at will from just after the spawn until early autumn. As sunlight hours shorten and water temperatures begin to fall, the same population of smallmouths feed on crayfish throughout the fall and winter months as their metabolisms dictate.

In addition to the crayfish and fish that comprise the staples of the smallmouth's diet, there are many other food forms that complete the menu. The frequency with which smallmouths feed on these prey depends on their availability. It might be seasonal abundance or just something that's a meal of opportunity taken only upon occasion.

Insect Meals

Mayflies, caddisflies, and stoneflies are a part of the small-mouth's diet in the insects' nymphal and adult forms. They are readily available and as attractive to smallmouths as they are to trout, but, since bass prefer slower water, presentations can be easier. Many anglers associate crayfish with smallmouth bass to the exclusion of insects and consequently in most waters they are under-utilized.

Damselflies, dragonflies, and dobsonflies are available in many smallmouth waters. Despite their slender appearance, damselflies can be a significant portion of the smallmouth's diet. Dragonflies are much larger and smallmouths are known to reck-lessly chase them. Especially in the adult form, these "Witch Doctors" hover above the water's surface like miniature helicop-ters. Smallmouths have been observed wildly leaping from the water to capture them. The nymphs are quick little creatures that dart about on silted bottoms until they are preyed upon by the bass. Dobsonflies' nymphal forms are called hellgrammites, which can be large and abundant in some waters. The hellgram-mite spends 3 years maturing to a length of 3 inches. They live under rocks and in rock crevices but they're capable of swim-ming through the water by flexing their bodies in an undulating movement. It's little wonder that hellgrammites are one of the smallmouths' favored foods.

Terrestrial insects are an important food source when they are seasonally available. In the summer when grasshoppers be-come abundant and active, smallmouths capitalize on them as an easily gulped food supply. The "hoppers" are nearly helpless when they land on water, where their desperate kicking attracts the attention of hungry fish.

Bottom Minnows

In addition to shad, shiners, chubs, young-of-the-year game-fish, and any of a wide variety of other free-swimming minnows, there are two baitfishes that hug the bottom and serve as primary food sources. Sculpin minnows inhabit the most oxygenated portion of streams. They are intolerant of pollution and are useful in gauging the health of our smallmouth waters where they are abundant. Imitations should be very heavily weighted and fished on sinking lines. Madtoms are another important food source. They look like miniature catfish and they are so attractive to smallmouths that we've had success with them in spring creeks at midday despite the preference of both fish for low light conditions. Madtoms prefer areas of slow current and usually are found over gravel- to cobblestone-sized rock.

Leeches

The leeches that inhabit many smallmouth waters swim along with an enticing wiggling motion. Their imitations should be fished close to weedbeds near the bottom with steady retrieves for best results. Each season leech patterns produce some smashing strikes from large smallmouths and should be a staple in every smallmouth angler's fly box. We prefer black-colored leech patterns, but natural-colored leeches in olive or gray are productive as well.

Frogs

Frog patterns account for many of our biggest smallmouths each year. From their first appearance at the water's edge in springtime until early fall they are fun to imitate with various presentations. They are replicated with small, size-8 cork poppers that are chugged across the surface or complex deer-hair ties that sit more realistically in the water rather than upon it.

Patterns that incorporate a Dahlberg-style head can be pulled under and made to swim a foot or two under water before resurfacing. Observe the naturals in the immediate area to mimic the frogs' size and coloration as well as their erratic action to entice smallmouth bass from weedbeds, grasses and deadfalls.

It's accurate to say that smallmouth fly-fishing is a little like trout fishing with some major differences, and it's equally correct that it's a little like largemouth bass fly-fishing with, again, some major differences. Without understanding and appreciating the unique character of this superb gamefish, many nuances of enjoyment are missed. This is the grandest of warmwater's sport fish with a tradition-rich history. Smallmouths are beautiful, adaptable, but highly selective. Their fights are frequently spectacular aerial displays that have been especially endearing to generations of long rodders. They are tenacious, relentless, and when finally brought to hand smallmouths glare in defiance through red eyes that seem to assert that they would win the next encounter.

CHAPTER 2
PREPARATIONS

Fly-fishing for smallmouth bass is as simple as taking a rigged-up fly rod and a handful of flies to the stream to wander down a graveled shoreline; however, most fly anglers choose to apply varying degrees of sophistication to our sport. The pleasure we derive from having just the right gadget or tool to do the job seems to increase our satisfaction with the total experience. Whatever approach is chosen, each piece of equipment should be carefully selected to serve its intended purpose.

Smallmouth bass reside in a wide variety of environments, from crystalline creeks one can step across to rocky, windswept submerged islands in the Great Lakes. Gear chosen with one of those places in mind would be entirely inadequate for the other. Here are some thoughts to consider when choosing gear for the variety of opportunities you may encounter.

Rods

Those confined to rod selection with budget constraints need to remain focused on the places they fish most often. In time, a wider range of rod weights and actions can be added to match different circumstances. Over the years we've spoken to many streamside philosophers, including guides, who have chosen a "smallmouth rod" for all their fishing. Not surprisingly, some swear by soft-action 5-weights while others can't bear the thought of smallmouth fly-fishing without their 7-weights. Lovers of diminutive spring creeks are quite comfortable with their 3-weight rods.

Philosophically speaking, we prefer to fish as light as we can. Rod choices should be made with regard to the size, weight, and wind resistance of the flies used with consideration for casting distance and the possibility of encountering wind. On small streams, where shorter casts are the rule and fly selections are relatively small and light, we like 3- or 4-weight rods. These light rods maximize the thrill of playing the fish. The memory of an 18-inch smallmouth bass pulling against our soft 8-1/2-foot 3-weight is very special. When casting match-the-hatch dries, drifting nymphs through riffles, or even when tossing weighted size-10 woolly buggers into pocket water, 3-weight outfits with floating lines seem just right. If sink-tip or full-sinking line is the choice, we switch to heavier rods. Obviously, these decisions are made before setting out if bank or wade fishing is the order of the day. Carrying two or more rods usually isn't practical unless watercraft is used.

The early years of our smallmouth fishing were spent with fiberglass rods. They were all we had in those days, and they didn't seem to inhibit fish-catching or our enjoyment of it, but today most of our rods are graphite. The exception is an exquisite 3-piece, 7-foot 4-weight split bamboo that casts so smoothly it seems to beckon each time we approach our rod rack. The marriage of cane rods and the most abundant native stream spe-

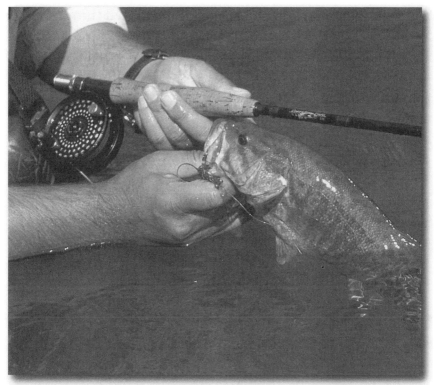

Five-, 6-, and 7-weight rods are excellent choices for the one-rod fly-fisher.

cies indigenous to North America offers a classic experience that traditionalists appreciate. Cane rods are heavier, generally slower, and often two to three times more expensive than top of the line graphite. On the other hand, they represent an investment that we would be proud to hand down to a grandchild when our last casts have been delivered.

Five, 6- and 7-weight rods make excellent choices for the one-rod smallmouth fly-fisher. Each rod can be delicate enough for subtle presentations while having enough backbone to handle heavier or more wind-resistant flies, stiff breezes or sinking fly lines. If we know the water we intend to fish, for example, pocket water perfect for casting small streamers, a 3-weight would likely be our choice. If a half-day trip or longer is on the agenda, it's likely that a variety of different situations will be encountered. Size-12 nymphs might be cast into riffles, and then weighted crayfish patterns might be drifted through pools of big rocks before casting Clousers into the shadows along steep bluffs. Floating lines are the logical choice in shallow runs, while sink-tip lines could be the best choice for deeper pools, and full-sinking lines can be necessary to get Clousers into the deeper portions of bluff holes. Five-, 6- or 7-weight rods handle each of these situations with ease. If size-6 or larger cup-faced poppers or deer-hair bugs figure into the plan, 7-weights can handle the variety of fishing situations best. Some excellent smallmouth fly-fishers, including guides, swear by 7-weights for all around versatility because the rods are capable of delivering their flies on target with few false casts. With adaptability as the key characteristic, we couldn't agree more, and we deviate from the mainstream only to enhance the thrill of playing these combative fish on lighter tackle.

Huge reservoirs harbor some wonderful smallmouth fishing, but big water can be exposed to the wind, and larger, heavier flies might be necessary. Many reservoirs with smallmouth bass in them are also very clear, which requires longer casts to prevent spooking the fish. Tackle for these trips should include 6-, 7- and 8-weight rods. Again, flies and conditions should determine the choice of rods. While we are advocates of selecting the lightest rod possible for the fishing situation, it must be remembered that nothing is more discouraging than trying to cast a lead-laced 1/0 fly into a stiff breeze using a rod with inadequate backbone.

Length is another aspect of rod selection well worth consideration. Shorter rods are at their best in small streams where overhanging branches lurk in the canopy waiting to grab flies and tippets. A 7- to 7-1/2-foot rod might be the best choice for this fishing, but for boat fishing from a seated position a longer rod will cast much more comfortably. Nine- to 9-1/2-foot rods are good choices. Our smallmouth rods range from 7 to 9 feet in rods of 3-, 4-, and 5-weights. The 6- to 8-weight rods are 8-1/2 to 9 feet.

Reels

Smallmouth bass are noteworthy fighters to be sure, but it's rare for one to run any great distance, so spool capacity isn't an overriding consideration when selecting a reel. The qualities we look for include durability, light weight, interchangeable spools, and smooth, adjustable drags.

We have owned reels that wore so badly with use that their spools wobbled. Like most other cheap items, low-end reels are poor choices for frequent use. Conversely, we have some older, high-quality reels that, despite their rough appearance, remain quite functional.

Lightweight reels are more desirable when matched with graphite fly rods. They provide better balance that gives the angler better control of the rod, which not only enhances casting pleasure but accuracy as well. Most quality reels today are 3 to 6 ounces, yet they are more durable than inexpensive heavyweights.

Changing spools is necessary for the versatile smallmouth fly angler and should be a quickly and easily performed operation. It's a good idea to carry one or two spare spools loaded with different lines. Some days several spool switches are necessary to keep flies in the fish zone. If switching from floating to sink-tip line were a difficult or time-consuming proposition, anglers might be apt to stick with whatever fly line they're using at the time and restrict themselves to poor, likely unproductive, presentations.

Small fish can be landed simply by stripping line, but larger fish should be put on the reel. It prevents loose, snarled line from costing the fly-fisher a wonderful memory and enhances the pleasure of the experience. Most times larger smallmouths will make quick, usually short, dashes for freedom that cause line to be pulled from the reel. If the drag is set too lightly or requires varying degrees of tension that results in a jerking spool rotation, the tippet can be easily snapped.

Automatic reels that retrieve line at the touch of a button were popular with bass fishermen in the 1950s and 1960s but have since lost favor among fly anglers. At that time, they were matched with heavy fiberglass rods but their heavy weight doesn't team up with modern graphite very well. In addition, their spare spools are time consuming to change.

Generally, fuss-free, simple fly-fishing gear that requires little maintenance is preferred. Reels are no exception. Single-action reels with adjustable drags that offer exposed spool rims to give further control when line is taken by a scrappy bronze-back are favored. By placing the palm of your free hand on the exposed spool rim you can vary the pressure instantly to brake a fish headed for a brush pile or allow a run into unobstructed water. Enough spool capacity to accommodate plenty of backing is a good choice, not because a smallmouth might run great distances, but because backing fills out the spool so that the line is stored in larger, less problematic curls while enabling more line to be retrieved with each turn of the reel handle. A large arbor reel performs well for the same reasons.

Lines, Leaders, and Tippet

Delicacy isn't normally a primary consideration in small-mouth fishing. While we don't want sloppy casts or bullet-like splashdowns, standard weight-forward tapers will handle most floating-line situations. Special bass bug tapers have shorter, heavier front tapers and are preferable when casting large, heavy or wind-resistant flies. We usually arm our lighter rods from 3- to 6-weights with regular weight-forward lines and rig the 7- and 8-weights with bass bug tapers. We use floating lines about fifty percent of the time, especially in smaller streams, but use them substantially less in stillwater.

We use sink-tip line about 25 percent of the time. Deep or fast stream sections, where getting the fly 3 to 5 feet deep is desired, or casting to the first drop-off in lakes requires moderately-fast sinking sink-tip lines. The one we like for smallmouth fishing has a sinking portion of 7 to 15 feet. Our favorite has a sink rate of 3 to 4 inches per second.

In water deeper than 5 feet, the use of a fast full-sinking line gets the job done best. The line gets flies down to the fish quickly, and because all of the line sinks at an even rate the retrieve is more horizontal than retrieves with either floating or sink-tip lines. This asset is helpful when presenting crayfish patterns or imitating bottom-hugging minnows like sculpins. Although there are some very fast sinking lines on the market, we prefer lines rated for 4 to 6 I.P.S. Full-sinking lines can be difficult to control in fast current where there are large obstructions such as boulders or downed trees and casting positions are limited. Sink-tip lines are less frustrating to use in this situation.

While we prefer separate spools loaded with floating, sink-tip, and full-sinking lines, there is another option. Most line manufacturers offer three or four line tips that are interchangeable using loop-to-loop connections to a running line. Having multiple tips enables the angler to utilize a floating tip, a slow sinking tip, and a fast sinking tip with one fly line. The cost of most multi-tip lines is roughly double that of single lines, but less than purchasing three or four single lines and the expense of spare spools is eliminated as well. Using different lengths of full-sinking line, we experimented with making our own multi-tip system several years ago. It was serviceable, but we disliked the hinging that occurred with the cast. It's a good idea to cast both options at a fly shop before making the choice.

When selecting floating fly lines we prefer to use lines rated one size heavier than the rod. For example, a 6-weight line on a 5-weight rod causes the fly rod to load easily and utilizes its flex to a greater extent. With sink-tip and full-sinking lines, that's not necessary because their increased weight loads the rod. An extra line size would slow the rod's action too much. Although overloading the rod is our personal preference, we advise experimentation with different line sizes at your local fly shop before your purchase. You'll soon know which rod and lines feel most comfortable for your casting stroke. It's also a good idea to clip the hook point off a couple of your most bedraggled flies of different weights to make your rod and line testing more realistic. It doesn't make sense to cast a line without the flies you like to use in actual fishing situations.

As the final connection between the angler and the imitation used to fool the fish, leaders must be used correctly. The problem is that there are so many variables. Leaders should be selected with regard to length, strength, and suppleness, and each must be matched to the fly and the situation in which it is fished. If the leader's butt section is too light or too supple, a heavy or wind-resistant fly will cause the line and leader to collapse in mid flight and land in a tangled pile that would fool few fish. By the same token, unnecessarily heavy tippet will restrict the fly's action and can be so bulky that it's noticeable to the fish.

Still, the process of selecting the right leader and tippet doesn't need to be unduly complicated. Here are the criteria we use. When using floating line for surface flies, use shorter leaders of 4 to 7-1/2 feet. The heavier or bulkier the fly, the heavier leader butt and tippet used. The clearer the water, the lighter the tippet and the smaller or sparsely tied the fly. Nymph and streamer fishing are best with longer leaders, usually 7-1/2 to 9 feet. They must be heavy enough to turn the fly over efficiently but supple enough to allow the fly to move freely. With sinking line, we use short leaders of 2-1/2 to 6 feet on lightly weighted imitations and longer leaders of 7 ½ to 9 feet on flies that are fished off the bottom. In this fishing situation, the light flies and long leaders are pulled downward when sinking lines are stripped. It should be recognized that a long leader on a sinking line with a lightly weighted fly tends to defeat the purpose of weighted line because the fly buoys toward the surface and the resulting slack line makes strike detection and hook-setting difficult. Still, it's a tactic that can be employed to move fish that are otherwise diffi-cult to interest. Long leaders are effective with heavily weighted flies because they do not arch toward the surface.

Tippet material can be radically different from brand to brand, especially with regard to suppleness. Again, it's important to match suppleness to the fly. A small diameter, high tensile strength fluorocarbon tippet might be the perfect match for nymphs drifted through riffles but it couldn't accommodate cup-faced poppers tossed toward graveled shorelines.

Carry a variety of leader lengths and strengths. Four-foot to 12-foot leaders with tippets from 0X to 6X should cover most any situation from high, stained water in early spring to low, exceptionally clear still water in mid-summer. Lots of anglers invest in top of the line rods and reels rigged with top-quality fly lines but become miserly with their leaders. Every time leaders make contact with rocks, branches, and vegetation they become abraded and therefore weakened. Weakened leaders won't hold fresh knots for attaching tippets and certainly won't hold strong, unpredictable smallmouths.

In fertile waters within the smallmouth's domain, leader shyness isn't much of a factor, but in the low water conditions of the winter season and in clear spring creeks we have encoun-tered the problem. One of our spring creeks sometimes runs milky. When it does, we get by with using 4X tippets, but when it's low and clear we're forced to use 6X tippets to reduce the number of refusals.

Knots

Many books have been written about the enormous numbers of knots that the fisherman can use. Most anglers feel they've lost too many good fish to poorly tied or unwisely selected knots. That's reason enough to take the subject seriously. It's better to select the correct knot for the job and focus on tying it correctly, rather than having a passing familiarity with a large number of knots. Our repertoire is a short list of knots that we've come to trust because they've performed well for us.

Most sources recommend using a nail knot to join the leader to the fly line. It's a good choice, but if you fish often you might change leaders countless times. In that case, you can add a perfection loop to the section that is attached to the fly line so that leaders can be attached easily, or attach braided loops sealed with superglue. Both wear and loosen with use, so whether nail knot, nail-knotted monofilament loop or braided loop is applied check it before each outing. At one time or another, all have been known to fail.

A surgeon's knot tied with a large loop in the leader's butt end allows fly-fishers to quickly remove or attach leaders even when there's very little light, such as sunrise and sunset or under a dense canopy of leaves on an overcast day. Fishing time is just too precious to make changing leaders a long, drawn out process.

An ordinary blood knot is excellent for joining tippet material to the leader. It's important to choose leader and tippet materials that are compatible. Stiff leaders need to be joined to stiff tippet material, for example.

When attaching the fly we again take a simple approach. Most often we use the improved clinch knot because it's very reliable even with large, heavy flies. Be certain to wet knots before pulling them tight. Dry ones pull apart or break easily; wet knots pull down tighter and don't slip as readily. From experience we know the smallmouth's environment is murder on knots. Rocks, gravel, and woody structure quickly weaken monofilament and the strain of pulling on lines and flies to free hang-ups can loosen knots. Always check loops and knots at regular intervals while fishing.

Some Thoughts On Hooks

Selecting a hook to use in tying flies for smallmouth bass isn't easy. A hook with a wider gap has a better chance to penetrate and hold the fish. So a wide-gap hook like a Mustad 37187 or TMC 8089 would be a good choice, but they aren't adequate for most nymphs and streamers. A hook with a round bend such as TMC 5262 is often a good choice. We especially like this hook for Clousers and crayfish patterns because the fly will ride hook point up when barbell eyes are attached. That's a great advantage in rocky, snag-filled waters, but when the fly is tied to ride in conventional fashion the same hook tends to hang up much too frequently. We prefer a hook with a limerick bend and a straight eye such as a TMC 200R for flies that will be fished hook point down. All of these hooks are barbed, but some can be purchased barbless, such as the TMC 200R-BL. It's a good idea to debarb the others.

Generally, smallmouths prefer smaller food forms than their greedy "bucket-mouthed" cousins. For most stream situations, flies of sizes 10 through 4 easily get the most use. In lakes and large rivers, big flies tend to prevail. Hook sizes 6 to 2 dominate lake fly boxes and the use of wide-gap hooks discourages constant attacks from bluegills and other sunfish.

Tackle-Carrying Options

When fishing from a boat or canoe we prefer to use a boat bag capable of carrying twelve fly boxes and leaders, tippet material, sunscreen, and all the paraphernalia we might need. However, if wade fishing is the assignment, there are several viable options. Traditionalists like to use vests. They hold lots of tackle, which allows the security of knowing that we'll usually have what we need. They can be heavy, however, and on hot summer days vests can feel suffocating. Traveling light is a good plan for long, hot wades and there are a variety of tackle packs that have become standard for lots of anglers and their guides. The real issue depends on how much gear you feel you need to carry with you on the stream.

Waders, Boots, and Gravel Guards

Waders are an essential part of the river smallmouth fly-fisher's gear. We prefer lightweight breathable stocking foot-chest waders. For us, they are the most comfortable and we can use them through the winter months by layering our clothing. In late spring and early autumn when the air is quite warm but the water is not, we find the long walks along big gravel bars less taxing with waders that aren't insulated. Stocking foot models allow the use of the boots alone while wet wading during the warmest part of the year. Felt soled boots are a must in the rocky streams most smallmouths inhabit; boots with studded soles or cleats can be helpful.

Rocky streams can be hard on waders. Gravel that finds its way over boot tops is terribly uncomfortable and wears holes in the stocking feet quickly. Gravel guards are inexpensive solutions to the problem, whether wearing waders or wading wet. It should be noted that waders often come with gravel guards attached, so the purchase of a separate pair may be unnecessary.

Wader Belts, Wading Staffs, and Inflatable Suspenders and Vests

Wading in rock-filled smallmouth streams can be treacherous. A misstep or slippery rock can end the day or worse, result in a serious injury. Fortunately, we've been able to avoid the latter, but we have ended a number of early- and late-season trips with accidental dunkings in cold water. A wader belt, tightened around the waist, can prevent the waders from filling too quickly and should be considered a necessity.

Most of our spills could have been prevented if we had supported ourselves long enough to regain our balance. A wading staff, whether improvised or store-bought is a good idea especially when wading unfamiliar water. If you dislike carrying a wading staff, an inflatable vest or inflatable suspenders offers the most viable safety option.

Sunglasses

Sunglasses with polarized lenses are essential to sight fishing, finding fish-holding structure, and viewing bottom contours and composition. Detection of water depth by sight would be impossible without them. In addition, they provide eye protection from errant backcasts or missed hook-sets.

Hook Disgorger/Pliers

As a preeminent gamefish, smallmouth bass should not be at risk when the hook is being removed. A pair of surgical forceps, available in most fly shops, allows the angler to gently remove even deeply taken flies. The same tool also serves in debarbing hooks, which enables the release of more fish unharmed and provides easier penetration on the hook-set.

Tape Measure

Whether wading, floating, or fishing from a boat, we always keep a tape measure handy. By placing a particularly nice fish alongside the rod while it's still in the water, then quickly releasing the fish we can measure its length on the rod's butt section. We feel this is the best method of judging and appreciating the size of the fish without putting it through the stress of excessive handling.

Inflatables

We began using float tubes in the early seventies with a heavy molded plastic model that allowed us to fish ponds and lakes that had no boat launches and offered few casting opportunities from their banks. We found we could fish so comfortably and quietly that we've since owned several inflatable float tubes.

Today there are a variety of styles that range from inexpensive donut-shaped tubes without many frills to user-friendlier U-shaped tubes complete with carrying handles, storage compartments, hooked-tape rod holders, and rulers for measuring the catch. There are also inflatables that allow anglers to sit above the water while their finned feet dangle into the water for propulsion. Battery operated, double action hand pumps, and small air compressors that operate by plugging into the cigarette lighter of your vehicle are widely available. The new generation of inflatables are easy to use, silent to operate, and as comfortable as fishing from your favorite easy chair. They can be used for fishing short stretches of slower river pools and for fishing isolated structure on big lakes, but a few words of caution should be noted. First, it is illegal to operate an inflatable without a Coast Guard approved life vest. Second, you should always tube with a partner. Finally, don't attempt to anchor in moving water. The anchor can easily become lodged in rocks or a root wad and drown the tube's occupant.

Many smallmouth rivers with lots of good pocket water are simply too rugged to make wading them a rewarding experience. Some can be fly-fished from canoes when there's enough water to make floating downstream without colliding with rocks practical, but inflatable rafts are often the more reasonable alternative. They draw surprisingly little water while offering maneuverability and comfort.

Canoes

Many consider canoeing smallmouth rivers a classic experience. We agree, and have included several canoe floats in our smallmouth fishing plan each season for many years. Canoes are light enough to portage around obstacles like dams and falls or into remote lakes. They are capable of a leisurely drift and

Many consider canoeing smallmouth rivers a classic experience.

Kevlar. These canoes can be expensive, but they set in, rather than on, the water, which makes them much more stable. They quietly glide over shoals with the ease of a snake and are exceptionally resistant to damage from collisions with rocks.

Kayaks

As fly-fishers sought personal watercraft for streams and lakes, kayaks became popular. They are valued for their stability, a critical characteristic for casting, light weight, maneuverability, and their ease in handling narrow runs in streams. They draw little water, which is a great advantage in shallow water.

Other River Craft

Jon boats offer another option to river floaters where there's enough water to glide over shoals. Many river guides use them because they offer stability and therefore greater safety for their inexperienced clients. One guide we've fished with has a 14-foot jon boat customized for float fishing. There are rod racks just under the gunnels on each side of the craft. The floors, without ribs, accommodate the standing caster. He controls the drift of the boat with a short-handled paddle from the stern but also uses a long-handled paddle and a push pole when they are needed. The boat is also equipped with a marine battery and a powerful electric trolling motor. It's used only to motor back to the head of a pool to fish a particularly productive piece of water and to navigate through unproductive water quickly. There's also plenty of room for a cooler to provide a bountiful shore lunch.

An eastern guide we know uses a 16-foot cataraft. His craft consists of two large inflatable pontoons and a lightweight frame that holds seating for three as well as a full load of gear. Oars in the midsection provide control and the craft has the advantage of sliding over shallow boulders and shoals so the seated anglers can take full advantage of pocket water and slow pools with a quiet approach.

For larger waters, McKenzie Drift Boats are the choice of most guides and experienced river travelers. They offer great stability in rough water, are highly maneuverable in moving water, and allow the standing caster all day opportunities.

Bass Boats

For lake fishing, modern high-tech bass boats meet the needs of fly-fishers. They provide two stable, spacious casting platforms and comfort for all-day fishing. On the negative side, most boats have too many exposed knobs, handles, and cables that seem to grab every loose coil of fly line.

Now that we understand our quarry and have the right gear, let's go fishing.

CHAPTER 3
PRESENTATION STRATEGIES

How many times have you observed another angler catch fish after fish while you've gone without a hit? Perhaps you even inquired about the angler's choice of flies, tied on his pattern, and continued to go fishless. Often, we simply conclude that the other guy has incomparable skill. Maybe, but it's more likely he's happened across just the right combination of approach, delivery, and fly animation.

While guiding canoe expeditions into the Boundary Waters Canoe Area north of Ely, Minnesota in the early 1970's, Terry encountered another guide who had lassoed a pointed rock at the end of a lake where the water swept into a river. The rope held his canoe steady as he and his client cast white jigs down and across the quickening current. In thirty minutes the two landed more than 20 smallmouths with many exceeding 15 inches. Their approach wasn't the only ingredient in their successful formula. Their angled casts enabled the jigs to swing across the current and gain depth along the way. As the jigs reached the end of the drift, the anglers lifted then lowered their rod tips repeatedly, which caused the lures to dart about like minnows trying to escape the current. The tactic was absolutely lethal, of course, but more importantly it was a dramatic demonstration of the importance of piecing together the puzzle of approach, delivery, and animation properly. Subsequently, Terry's large streamers worked as well as their jigs. Solving the mystery of approach, delivery, and fly animation is clearly the difference between catching lots of fish and catching none.

Bank Stalking

In many lakes and along most rivers, it's difficult to cover a substantial amount of water from the bank. But while casting opportunities can be limited, the bank-stalking approach is fly-fishing's simplest form. Armed only with a fly rod, reel, line, and a few flies, an angler can capitalize on the casting positions that can be reached along the shore.

Bank fishing requires some forethought for gratifying results. Brightly colored clothing and reflective sunglasses are ill advised. Smallmouths are generally found in relatively clear water, which tends to amplify the problem of being seen by the fish. Similarly, a noisy approach is certain to put these cautious fish on red alert. Drab-colored or camouflage clothing coupled with a quiet, careful approach is important for consistent success. On streams that are heavily used by boaters and canoeists, anglers often find the fish are so accustomed to noise and commotion on the surface that they return to feeding again within minutes of passing canoes or outboard motors.

Keep the angle of the sun in mind when selecting a casting site. Shadows from the angler's body or even the rod and line can send every smallmouth in casting range into the depths with a severe case of lockjaw. Seek out areas where a breeze ripples the water. Your approach will be less detectible there than in areas of mirror-smooth water.

Utilize brush, tall grass or bankside obstructions to break up your outline and shield you from the fish's view. Keep a low profile, kneeling whenever possible. It's also helpful to minimize false casts as the continuous motion increases the risk of eventually being spotted by the ever-alert bass. Repetitious false casting also increases the chances of either rippling the water on the forward cast or hooking brush or grass on the backcast. Either mistake can spook wary fish.

Advanced planning regarding the approach to a stationary casting position minimizes scared fish. Walking along the exposed shoreline handicaps your efforts; therefore, try to select a route that will allow you to begin casting without detection from a location that enables the coverage of several different targets. Sloppy casts and hang-ups can short-circuit the whole process, but common sense can overcome self-defeating approaches.

Wading fly anglers have more flexibility in their choices of casting positions.

Wading

Wading allows a fly-fisher to take a position that ensures the most advantageous presentation of the fly while reducing the likelihood of hang-ups on the backcast. Many fishermen wade carelessly through the best water spooking fish, destroying habitat, and silting downstream areas unnecessarily. This momentary thoughtlessness sabotages their objectives but the oversight can be remedied with some advanced planning.

In moving water, the first decision that needs to be made is whether to fish upstream or down. Knowledge about the stretch of stream in question is necessary to make the best choice. If you fish there regularly, it will make the decision easy. If not, a reconnaissance walk along the bank in both directions will provide the needed information. It's helpful to know where the head of the pool is located, its length, depth, and whether or not it's shaded. If there is a plunge pool, there will likely be a "lip" that could hold big fish. Next, look at the size, depth, current speed, and composition of the body of the pool. Notice how sunlight affects the pool. Is it wadable? If so, what is the safest, most productive wading path that will provide the least disturbance to the fish? Look for fish hangouts such as undercut banks, bluffs, mid-pool boulders, and deadfalls. If it's unwise to wade through the entire pool, it's important to locate places to get out of the water to circumvent the problem area. Finally, scout the tail of the pool to look for adequate cover. Check out the current speed and depth, and look for a dramatic rise from the streambed into the shallower tailout. This "lip" may provide the most productive portion of the entire pool.

When scouting is complete, the angler can determine where and how to fish the water based on the variables of season, weather, water clarity, and light penetration. If, for example, it's spring and the water is 2 to 4 inches higher than normal and a bit off color, you may choose to wade into midstream and cast toward the shallow gravel bars on either side of the river. But if it's a warm summer afternoon with the water low and clear, you may want to seek out the depth of a bluff pool below the entrance point of a spring.

If advance knowledge of the water isn't possible, it's usually best to fish downstream simply because the current will assist with fly manipulation. By choosing flies such as streamers that can be maneuvered effectively in the current you can be more certain of an effective presentation. Upstream presentations are effective only when line can be retrieved quickly enough to keep slack removed. If the current is too swift, removing slack line quickly enough is impossible and strikes are rarely detected. The disadvantage of fishing downstream is that silt or debris kicked up by wading is washed into the vicinity of the angler's next cast and may very well disturb the fish. Upstream fishing offers the possibility of getting the fly deeper into the water column and also facilitates a drag-free drift.

Wading stillwater must be confined to areas where there's enough shallow water with a firm, wadable bottom. Usually this limits the fly-fisher to short stretches of shoreline and also limits the productivity of those areas to spring spawning sites or low light conditions. The same problems we enumerated for the bank-bound stillwater angler apply to the wading fisherman, but there is an additional hazard. Unless you know the water very well, it's easy to step off into a deep hole.

We pursue smallmouths year around, and most of our wade fishing is done in waders. But when the weather gets hot, quick-drying shorts and a pair of wading boots is a hard combination to beat. Empty the pockets of your shorts and stow your billfold and car keys in a sealed plastic bag, then secure the waterproof package in a breast or vest pocket. Our advice is especially applicable to those with remote keyless entry devices. This is the voice of experience speaking.

Whether bank-bound or wading, precise casting positions for stationary presentations are limited by the depth of the water. Wading anglers have more flexibility thus the choices of stationary casting positions may be critical to success. Often we've observed fishermen who position themselves directly across the stream from the structure they intended to fish irrespective of current speed or fly choice. Usually this miscalculation results in an almost nonexistent drift and, consequently, only the slightest chance for a hook-up. It may also fail to take the content of the river bottom into consideration. If sand, silt or mud is present, the result of wading that stretch could adversely affect further attempts at fishing downstream.

It's also short sighted to wade through productive water if it can be avoided. By driving the fish in the section farther downstream, it may well alert the newly encountered fish of the fisherman's presence. If the spot that you've chosen as the next casting position looks productive, fish the area before wading into it.

Fishing From Watercraft

Any watercraft, whether it's a float tube, canoe, kayak, jon boat or fully equipped bass boat, can serve the purpose of facilitating the delivery of the fly. All are capable of moving the angler into a variety of positions for stationary casting but that's not the only available delivery choice. Drifting, controlled drifting, and trolling are also possible.

A successful delivery system displays the fly to the fish so that it results in a strike. For this to happen consistently, it's necessary to maximize the length of time our fly spends in the fish zone. Most often this is a depth that takes water temperature, sunlight penetration, cover or structure, and the presence of forage targeted by the smallmouth population into account. If we can determine, either through experimentation or use of an electronic fish locator, which conditions are holding our intended quarry we can then devise a delivery system capable of keeping our fly at that depth and near that structure. This might mean maneuvering our watercraft into a position that enables us to cast over the structure and count down our offering to the appropriate depth. Counting, "one thousand-one, one thousand-two" and so on, can accomplish this until the fly reaches the desired depth. It's necessary that we know the sink rate of the fly, and that on floating line the leader is long enough to accommodate the drop. One person's count will differ from another's, but as long as we know that our imitation arrives at the targeted depth at our specific count, we can return to that depth consistently. To know the sink rate of a particular fly, simply observe its descent through clear stillwater.

In knowing that a rock hump that's within 4 feet of the surface is holding smallmouths, we can cast over the rock pile and count our fly to a depth of 4 feet before beginning the retrieve. Each time the fly is moved, it travels toward the rod tip and therefore it must be counted down again to the desired depth before the next strip is imparted. The length of the second countdown is dependent upon the length of the retrieve. If the fly sinks at a rate of 6 inches per second, for example, we might cast across the rock hump, count the fly down 8 counts, then lift the rod tip 2 feet and count the fly down again this time for 4 counts.

Another delivery system option is using the force and direction of the wind to push our craft across the aforementioned rock hump. This drifting technique depends, of course, on the speed and direction of the wind. If both are correct, it can be a successful presentation. Frequently, however, the wind pushes us too slowly, too rapidly or off course. When this happens we can correct our course and speed by turning an electric trolling motor on and off as needed. This is known as controlled drifting. The method utilizes the wind and yet allows the angler to stay on track with the presentation. If the wind is completely wrong or nonexistent, continual use of the electric motor, or trolling, may be necessary to control the speed and depth of the fly. Any of these delivery systems can be performed with electric or gas motors, oars, fins or foot paddles.

Canoes and jon boats are traditional river craft for float fishing, which enables anglers to reach choice smallmouth bass water. When float fishing streams we find beaching the canoe for wade fishing most productive, but there are lots of fish-holding pools that are too deep or too treacherous to wade. In these situations the angler in the bow seat does the fishing while the angler in the stern handles the canoe unless the current is slow enough to enable casts by both. We assess the pool's potential in consideration of current, structure, shade, and forage possibilities then plan 3 passes through it. The first pass is made parallel to and a moderate distance from the area that's most likely to hold the largest fish. If the pool is located in a river bend, completing the necessary evaluation of the pool's potential casting targets without spooking all of the smallmouth population is performed on this first pass. Streamers and attractor patterns that enter the water softly and do not cause excessive disturbances are carefully cast and retrieved while watching for fish activity. If the fly is followed but not taken, it's important to note the origin of fish's approach. If the fish comes from deeper water our next pass will be directed to get flies deeper into the water column. Often this means repositioning the canoe so that presentations can best cover deep water. Heavily weighted crayfish patterns and Clousers are good choices in this situation. If the bass respond from shallow cover our fly choices are surface poppers or floater/divers on the second pass. Whether or not a third pass is made is determined by the results from the first two. If we remain convinced there are catchable bass that have not been disturbed, we will pass through the pool once more while utilizing tactics and flies that create disturbances. Heavily weighted subsurface flies can be intentionally retrieved into rocks or wood structure or aggressively manipulated poppers can imitate struggling surface prey. These noisy retrieves are meant to interest fish that haven't responded to quieter presentations.

Casting

Various casts are useful to smallmouth fly-fishers. Conventional overhand forward casting with accuracy is fortunately the only ingredient necessary to enjoy the fight of this marvelous gamefish. Distance casts (haul and double haul) curve casts, reach casts, tuck casts, roll casts, and the gamut of available presentations do, without question, enhance the smallmouth bass chaser's chances of successfully coping with the myriad of conditions he is apt to face. Even those with modest fly-casting skills can and will catch bass. It just becomes more satisfying to develop advanced presentations and utilize them in the capture of fish.

The art of the stationary cast, in all its many forms, is a subject already covered in great detail by others in books and on videotape. It's not our intent to present a casting manual in these pages. If you feel you need a refresher course or would like to learn more advanced casting techniques, you can subscribe to fly-fishing magazines, invest in books or videos or seek out hands-on learning experiences through casting seminars at fly shops or fly-fishing shows. The practical smallmouth chaser will eventually need a varied arsenal of deliveries. The reason for this is that smallmouths take small nymphs and bulky wind-resistant poppers. Smallmouth bass are found under overhanging tree limbs, at the back of large eddies, and across currents of varying speeds. Floating line and surface flies might be needed in one situation or full-sinking lines and lead-laced flies in another.

We recommend the reach cast for moving water. As the fly line is straightening on the forward cast, reach across your body or to the side of your casting hand and point the rod tip upstream from the fly's splashdown site. The purpose of the reach cast is to provide a longer, drag-free drift in moving water. When it is used in combination with line-mending the fly-fisher can get a long, drag-free drift, and action can be imparted when the fly has reached its desired depth.

If a right-handed caster is fishing down and across the stream, for example, and the current is moving from right to left the fly should be cast at an angle downstream. As the fly line is unfurling, the casting arm and the rod tip should reach to the right, or upstream direction, from the fly's splashdown. See Illustration 3-A for an example of a right-handed fly-caster using a reach cast in current that moves from left to right. If the current moves left to right, the right-handed caster needs to reach across his body to point the rod tip upstream.

The angle at which such a cast is made is dependent upon the speed of the current. Experience will eventually teach the caster the best angles for a drag-free drift, but a novice should start by facing straight downstream if the stream flow is right to left and the shore is on the right. The angle between the direction

The reach cast assists a drag-free drift.

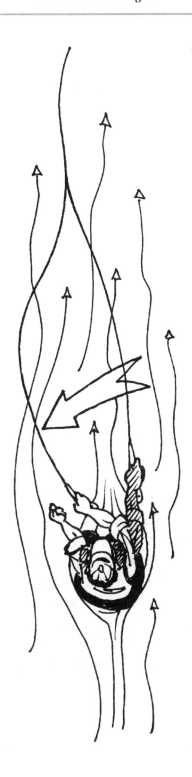

Illustration 3-A

the angler is facing and the shoreline, then would be 90 degrees. The angler should begin by turning his body to reduce the angle to 45 degrees. Make the cast at a target on that 45-degree angle and finish the cast by reaching to the right and pointing the rod tip another 30 degrees upstream. A moderately flowing current will allow the fly to drift drag-free for several feet before moving water causes the fly to swing in an arc downstream.

If the current is too fast to permit an adequate drag-free float, the angle must be increased, while slower current will enable the angle to be reduced. It's important to realize that the position of the caster is a variable that allows him to change the angle. There are other presentations, like the tuck cast, that are designed to give fly-fishers a drag-free float and enable the fly to get deeper, but for down-and-across fishing the reach cast is the simplest and most efficient.

Mending

One of the complications associated with fishing in current is that the water between the caster and the hook moves faster than the fly. When this happens, the belly of the fly line is pushed downstream first, which sweeps the fly off its intended course and pulls it awkwardly across the surface. The remedy for this problem is called mending. It's accomplished by using a looping motion of the rod tip to toss as much line as possible upstream without moving the fly. Use the rod tip to lift the slack line from the water then flick the rod hand upstream. It's important once this is accomplished to resume pointing the rod tip at the drifting fly and remove all slack line by stripping. If the slack is not removed, the fly will continue to drift downstream and when a strike occurs the angler will not be able to recover quickly enough to hook the fish. It's possible to achieve several mends on the same drift, thereby lengthening the drag-free float. Mending also allows wet flies to sink deeper before action is imparted. Many fly anglers forget how critical mending their casts can be when they fish from boats or canoes. Mending is as important to angling success when fly-fishing from watercraft as it is when wading.

Fly Animation

The angler must impart any fly movement that's independent of the current. Stripping is the most efficient method of retrieving the fly. It is accomplished by pinning the flyline against the rod between the index and middle finger of the rod hand and removing all slack line. Pull line with your line hand through your rod hand fingers. Point the rod tip at the fly and follow its movement as the current pushes it along. At the point you wish to impart action, repeat the stripping process. Normally, slow, short 2-inch strips followed by pauses will bring the most responses from the fish. Sometimes fast, erratic 6-inch or longer strips are necessary to provoke a strike. Consistent success often depends on finding the retrieve that triggers hits and repeating it until hook-ups begin to get scarce. That will signal the need to vary the retrieve.

Another viable option in animating the fly is allowing the current alone to move the fly, then temporarily interrupting the dead drift by lifting the rod tip then lowering it again. This moves the fly shallower and, in the process, creates slack. Lowering of the rod tip causes the fly to sink back toward the bottom. As it rises toward the surface, then sinks toward the bottom, the fly appears to be escaping. Hesitation means the aggressive smallmouth bass will miss an opportunity for an easy meal. This lifting action can trigger otherwise lethargic bass.

In slow water, some anglers prefer a hand-twist retrieve. Place the line hand across the top of the line with the palm facing down and grasp the line between the thumb and index finger. Next, rotate the line hand until the palm faces up, creating a loop, which can be grasped by the thumb and forefinger. Repeating the process will leave the line neatly coiled in your line hand and causes the fly to react with an enticing rocking motion.

The choice between stripping and hand-twist retrieves is largely a matter of personal preference, but whichever is employed the fly should be allowed to resettle after each pull. Both retrieves should be executed with the rod tip near the water's surface to facilitate the removal of slack line and provide a more direct connection between the rod and striking fish. If slack is present during the strike, the fish must hook itself and, as a result, most strikes will be missed.

It's easy to fall into the habit of imparting too much action to the fly. Subconsciously most of us theorize that if a little action is good, then more action is better. That's rarely the case. Carried to the extreme, constant imparted action causes the fly to flutter along near the surface. Most of the time a fly retrieved in this manner simply won't get deep enough in the water column to be a viable target for the bass.

A wet fly must fall through the water column. How it is controlled by the fly-fisher as it does so affects the fly's animation as well as its path into the fish's field of vision. One of the methods of fly animation for wet flies is the vertical drop. From the time the fly hits the water it is in a free fall toward bottom until it halts when all of the caster's slack line is pulled straight or until the fly actually comes to rest on the bottom. The amount of slack line that's needed depends upon the depth of the anticipated vertical drop. For the vertical drop to be attractive to the fish, the fly must be constructed so that it produces action or movement on its descent through the water column without any manual manipulation. Marabou, rubber hackle, and rabbit strips are three examples of materials that are flexible enough to accomplish this mission.

To fish the vertical drop effectively the fly-fisher must become a line watcher. Any twitch or hesitation should be answered with a hook-set. The falling fly appears to the bass to be wounded prey that's drifting helplessly into its lair, which presents a feeding opportunity that doesn't require much effort.

In addition to controlling the speed and vertical action of the fly, anglers can also control its direction. By pointing the rod tip to the right and stripping line, then shifting the rod tip position to the left and stripping again, the fly-fisher can change the path of the fly's movement. Bait casters have long employed this tactic for surface lures and call the technique "walking the dog." Fly-fishers recognize that they can use the same tactic to give their imitations that change-of-direction action. Flyline is more difficult to move in the water, however, and short casts on long leaders facilitate the maneuver's execution. The erratic action helps create the illusion that food is escaping while also simulating the natural action of nature's creatures in the water. To "walk-the-dog" use a pencil popper or other streamlined fly on the surface. An elongated body aids in pointing the lure in different directions.

The change-of-direction retrieve is effective with subsurface flies also. Because heavier sink-tip and full-sinking lines are difficult to move laterally this presentation should be considered only for relatively shallow water or still water when using floating line. Lengthening the leader facilitates maneuverability. The change-of-direction retrieve is most effective when it's used to make contact with the targeted structure. Structure bumping utilizes the bass's sense of hearing that helps them locate food in their environment. The idea is intentionally retrieving a fly into structure so that the noise will be audible to the fish, then changing directions and retrieving the fly away from the structure. This tactic can be further broken down into rock banging, stump knocking, and veggie bumping. Bass are accustomed to hearing prey make contact with their environment and can move toward an unseen prey to feed opportunistically. Stump knocking and veggie bumping are most effective in stillwater because the sound carries farther there. By intentionally stripping a fly into vegetation, it will frequently hook into the leaves or stems of plants. Usually a firm strip away from the vegetation is effective in freeing it. The sound and movement of the vegetation prompts the bass to search for the life form that caused it.

Rock banging, especially when performed using flies with heavy barbell eyes (Clousers, for example), makes a clicking sound when the fly contacts rocks. This is a particularly effective tactic when streams are stained from recent rains. Many times we have improved our success with rock banging after other retrieves were ignored. To execute structure bumping or rock banging, cast past the rock, stump, or weed clump and after the splashdown, move the rod tip so that the path of the fly will intercept the structure. Strip the line vigorously to achieve a solid collision, then change rod tip directions and strip the fly away. See Illustration 3-B for an example of the rock-banging technique. After the vertical drops, drag-free drifts, and variations of stripping retrieves fail; structure bumping will often activate the smallmouth population. It happened just that way one morning at sunrise on Missouri's Huzzah Creek.

Sunrise on the Huzzah

Nearly a decade ago, Terry and his brother "Lefty" spent a week wandering the back roads near the rural parsonages where their father had grown up 60 years before. A lifelong friend of their father's who grew hay and raised cattle owned a premier stretch of one of the region's best smallmouth rivers. The sun-baked farmer tilted his weather-beaten straw hat back exposing tired eyes as he pointed to the distant field road they could use to reach one of his pastures. They set up camp in a streamside grove of maples and sycamores and fell asleep to the sound of Huzzah Creek rushing past the rocks in its path.

At first light they sipped coffee from wire-handled tin cups while they vacantly stared at the flickering firelight to clear the cobwebs from their brains. In moments, the allure of the river overtook them and they crept into the stream in creamy morning light armed with 3-weights.

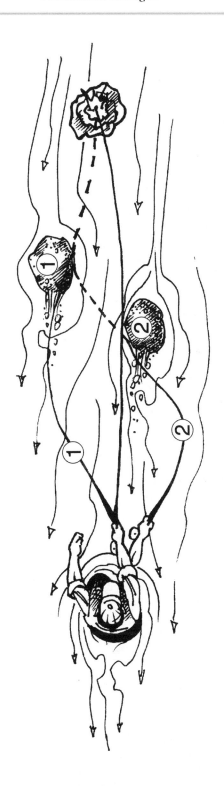

Illustration 3-B

A tan Woolly danced beside a deadfall but repeatedly failed to generate a single strike before a size-10 Clouser was put into service. A sidearm cast sent the offering under the protruding branches of a tree that had been uprooted and swept into the creek. Risking a possible hang-up, the fly was retrieved into the wood then allowed to drift freely for a couple of feet before Terry twitched the rod tip to bump into another solid branch. Only an instant later he flicked his wrist to set the hook on a smallmouth bass that put a deep bend in his 8-1/2-foot rod. A shower of bright water droplets glistened in the sunlight before the bronze rocket dug for the bottom. The tugs for dominance appeared to be a standoff for long minutes as the rod tip bounced rhythmically from the head-shaking movements of the angry bass. After two more leaps, then a few progressively shorter runs, the fish was brought to hand. Laying a rod alongside, he measured his catch. "Eighteen," his brother decided.

They smiled and nodded as the great fish finned into the depths.

By the time they had leapfrogged around a long riverbend the sun was above the trees and they strolled leisurely back to camp through the pasture still wet with dew. Perhaps 20 smallmouths had fallen for the same structure-bumping presentation while drifts past structure were ignored.

CHAPTER 4
STILLWATER

In 1970 we spent a week in a houseboat on the legendary waters of Dale Hollow Reservoir in northern Tennessee. Armed only with the knowledge that the world's record smallmouth bass had come from the lake in 1955, we had excitedly planned to make the trip with another couple whose enthusiasm for finding big smallmouths matched our own. We collected all the maps, shared all the pertinent magazine articles, and carefully packed every fishing contrivance we owned. Upon arrival, our enthusiasm increased to epic proportions because the lake truly looked like the world-class fishery we envisioned. We immersed ourselves in the quest for a gigantic bronzeback. Nonstop casting all of the first day produced nothing but fatigue, sunburn, and a couple of "might have been" hits. Swallowing our pride, we motored to the nearest marina in search of advice where a talkative tackle salesman drew a map for us. We rushed to his secret hole and again cast ourselves into depression with nothing to show but several sunfish and a very surprised white perch. Then we remembered the words of a grizzled, elderly whittler who had been seated in a rocking chair at the marina. "Fish them rocky points, and if you ain't hangin' up, you ain't gonna catch brown bass." Finally, we began to catch a few fish, although the new world record eluded us.

Two years later, Terry made his first trip into the Boundary Waters Canoe Area north of Ely, Minnesota. Again, he had heard the North country bass stories, had read all the pertinent articles he could find, and this time had consulted veteran guides before heading out with marked maps. He couldn't wait to reach his destination to set up camp so he could fish. Every piece of water he paddled was postcard gorgeous with classic smallmouth structure littering the landscape. Truly, he had reached the smallmouth fisher's Valhalla. An hour after the first cast, his only hook-ups were the backsides of rocks. Fuelled only by his enthusiasm, he paddled along the shoreline occasionally pausing long enough to make random casts toward the banks, an approach that proved to be a miserable failure. While the water temperature felt cool to his touch (he had no temperature gauge in those days) it was mid-July and the spawn was just past. It was also mid-afternoon and sunlight exposed every pebble and crevice on the shallow flats. Once again, his exuberance had persuaded him that the long anticipated destination would produce fabulous fishing and any cast that hit the water would fool a fat and sassy bronze rocket. It finally dawned on him that, just like the waters at home, he'd have to think his way through the fish location puzzle. Eventually, he discovered cooperative smallmouth bass scattered among piles of rocks at the base of a shaded bluff. Once found, they rose to poppers and smashed streamers enthusiastically, which kept his glass rod bent and his campfire instant replays lively.

Two different bodies of stillwater, one a mid-South impoundment, the other a Canadian border natural lake, taught him the same lesson about lake fly-fishing for smallmouth bass. It is locating smallmouth bass, not fooling them into striking, that's the challenge. In both these different situations he found large populations of smallmouth bass willing to strike almost any-thing, but he also discovered large areas of great-looking struc-ture that were totally devoid of the species. Eventually we would learn that finding one successful area didn't necessarily mean that we could fish similar structure in the same lake under the same conditions and expect to catch fish.

Smallmouths are largely regarded as homebodies, and while this is generally true in summertime streams, it is anything but true in northern natural lakes, southern impoundments or even in huge river systems that resemble stillwater. Sprawling major rivers like the St. Lawrence or the upper Mississippi offer numer-ous forage possibilities and diverse structural opportunities that tend to cause pods or schools of the same year-class smallmouth bass to move from area to area and from one forage species to another. In big waters, smallmouths are very nomadic not only as seasonal changes occur, but also within the same 24-hour peri-od. The reasons for their wanderlust include spawning, comfort, safety, and, we believe, most often the availability of their food sources. Their relocations could relate to the eventual scarcity of certain prey because the prey are so intensively utilized over time or possibly the smallmouths' need to change their diet. In the case of crayfish, for example, it's known this food source doesn't move about a lake to any substantial degree. Minnows, such as shad, on the other hand, do move about significantly.

Stillwater smallmouths are very adaptable, opportunistic, and mobile as meets their needs. These movements aren't random, nor do they encompass the whole lake. These periodic reloca-tions are to structure that has similar characteristics, perhaps with a shallow rock-strewn flat, initial breakline, and sometimes a relatively deeper breakline that offers the safety of deep water. The initial breakline is an area in which a gradually sloping bot-tom rapidly drops away into deeper water. In murky water, it is often the place where vegetation stops growing; in very clear water, sunlight penetration allows weed growth to continue to the secondary breakline. Within the regular relocation cycle we believe that there are also daily movements that usually occur in summer during periods of low light.

To understand the best locations to find smallmouths we need to review the requirements of smallmouth bass covered in Chapter One. In addition, we need to understand the differences between the types of lakes that harbor smallmouths. Natural lake smallmouths, for example, behave a little differently than their impounded brethren due to the effects of structure and competing species.

First let's look at the simplest of the stillwater situations: ponds. Ponds are differentiated from lakes only by their size, and can be natural or manmade. Most natural ponds are located in the northern portion of the smallmouth's range where temperatures can stay within tolerable limits for the species. Most southern ponds don't provide suitable habitat for smallmouths because their waters become too warm during the summer months. Only those ponds that are substantially spring-fed, in our experience, are possible smallmouth fisheries. Both types of ponds are rather easy to fish because the amount of structure in them is limited. Because the smallmouth bass cannot move about a great deal, a wider menu is accepted by these restricted populations. In ponds, presentation is the key to success.

Natural smallmouth bass lakes are mostly located along the northern tyer of states from New England across the Great Lakes states, and the southern portion of Canadian provinces through scattered lakes in the northwest where the bass were introduced long ago. Those lakes that are homes to smallmouth bass remain cool, at least in their deeper sections, throughout the summer. Most have rocky shorelines and hardwood forests interspersed with pines that usually occupy the surrounding landscape. These lakes are most often ringed with shallow weedlines, and often there are secondary weedlines at the first drop-offs into deeper water. The bottom content ranges from rock to sand and gravel. The body of the lake might include islands and submerged humps, which create situations that replicate the lake's shoreline in terms of bottom content and contour.

The water in these northern natural lakes is generally clear, but there are moderate amounts of mineral richness that lessen clarity yet enable plants and animals to prosper by feeding upon dissolved nutrients. These minute life forms attract and sustain larger minnows, sub-aquatic insects, and crustaceans, which, in turn, attract and sustain the smallmouth population. Lakes with only sparse nutrient enrichment may have a population of large smallmouths but they will be fewer in number than those in bodies of water where nutrients are abundant. Those waters that are low in nutrient productivity are called oligotrophic or scant nourishment lakes. These are very young lakes geologically.

The opposite in respect to geological aging is a very fertile, shallow lake with abundant weed growth. These old lakes aren't the most suitable smallmouth environments. New vegetation grows more rapidly than it decays. The lake, in this stage, is gradually becoming a bog.

Smallmouth bass prefer middle-aged lakes with moderate amounts of nutrients and vegetation. Smallmouths use graveled, shallow shoreline areas for spawning, but afterward abandon the areas for the first breaklines. Summers are spent in the areas between the first and second breaklines where the bass move either shallower or deeper within the zone in accordance with water temperatures, availability of forage species, intrusions by competing species, and sunlight penetration. They normally migrate daily for brief periods to forage in shallower areas, including shallow flats during low light conditions.

Within the same season smallmouths will, as previously noted, move from place to place as the availability of their prey becomes increasingly scarce. They might occupy an area of gravel mixed with chunk rock off the point of an island then suddenly seem to disappear only to turn up over a submerged hump half a mile away. Later they might be found between boulder-sized rocks below the first breakline. These migrations are at least predictable to some extent within wide parameters affected primarily by the weather. For example, good numbers of fish could be located off the point of the aforementioned island each July and along several mid-lake humps by early August, but if early July is unseasonably cool and rainy the fish might not gather there until later in the month.

In northern natural smallmouth lakes, it's our experience that bass scatter over a rather wide area after the spawn. This scattering period can last a couple of weeks and has been known to last up to a month, but it doesn't eliminate fishing for smallmouths. They remain active feeders during this transition period, but anglers must constantly change locations to find and catch them even after they begin to regroup in tighter schools. Late summer fishing, conversely, is normally focused on more concentrated schools of fish. It's often possible to catch good numbers of smallmouths from one location. Submerged rock islands and humps, rock piles along breaklines, and the bases of bluffs often serve as ambush points for these late summer fish. They forage heavily on minnows that they attack as the prey swim past the rocky structure. Their locations are harder to pinpoint during this period, but the fish-catching can accelerate once they're found. Electronic locators can be very useful in finding the breaklines and submerged humps favored by smallmouth bass.

It should be noted that spawning could take place in some of these areas from the middle of May through July. Obviously, checking water temperatures is an important element of the fishing plan during this period.

Finally, we should recognize that the smallmouths that inhabit many major rivers behave similarly to those in natural lakes. That is to say that their summer movements are subject to weather, structure, and prey movement as opposed to reacting to current and the constraints of relatively small pools, as are their stream-bound brethren. These massive rivers contain more diverse structure that offers the bass more options than populations that are more confined.

Impoundments provide much more diverse structural elements than natural lakes. Sprawling southern reservoirs can therefore be intimidating to fishermen, but long summers and tremendously fertile water enable some phenomenal smallmouth growth rates. It's no accident that the 11-pound, 15-ounce world record came from one such mid-South reservoir and it seems likely that the next behemoth will, too. Yet it's important to recognize that not all of these manmade lakes support a smallmouth bass fishery. In the mid-South, summer air temperatures and sunshine raise surface water temperatures into the tepid range. For smallmouths to survive and thrive there must be a source of cooling water or enough depth for the fish to remain cool throughout the hot summer months. The best of these reservoirs are steep-sided with rocky banks. Most are augmented by spring-fed rivers of substantial size, their waters are continuously released at their dams, and they have slight currents like the large rivers we alluded to previously.

While we recognize the importance of weed growth in an impoundment, particularly for the purpose of providing a safe haven for smallmouth fry, there are many lakes that qualify as excellent smallmouth fisheries where vegetation is either very sparse or nearly nonexistent. Hardwoods, cedars, and a few pines normally surround the best of these lakes, which also have many steep-sided coves. As in natural lakes, rocks of diverse sizes form the best areas. Gravel is important in the shallows for spawning, but chunk rock holds the best crayfish hideouts and also provides cover for foraging smallmouths. Other prominent forage species might include minnows, salamanders, frogs, young bullhead catfish, and young sunfish. Many of these reservoirs have rock bluffs that tower above the water. Those with stair step ledges and piles of rock of various sizes at their bases are smallmouth bass magnets.

There are many other kinds of structure in an impoundment that are used by smallmouths. Riprap along the face of the dam, bridge approaches, and wave breaks that protect marinas provide good foraging areas for bass. Old roadbeds and stone or concrete building foundations can be equally attractive structures.

The nutrient-rich, but generally clear, water preferred by smallmouth bass can pose some presentation problems. In our experience the clearer the water, the more sparsely flies should be tied. Even normally dressed imitations appear so bulky that they often scare the scales off the bass. This lesson was driven home to Terry nearly fifty years ago in the crystalline waters of Lake Superior. The water was so clear at such great depths that he could see his flies and watch fish react to them. At the time he didn't understand the concept of tying sparsely, but he found that the only way he could induce hits from the smallmouths was by using the wet fly patterns his family's host used in the area's brook trout streams. Today we might fish the same situation with full-sinking line, a 9-foot leader with a 5X tippet and size-8 or –10 very sparsely tied Clousers with extra small barbell eyes.

Seasonal Use Areas

Putting together a smallmouth seasonal movement chart is problematic. Fish in colder climates tend to respond at lower temperatures than those in southern impounds where surface temperatures can reach 90 degrees. We speculate that lengthening or shortening periods of daylight are factors in prompting the seasonal movements of fish as well.

We have noticed smallmouth movements toward the shallows in northern lakes when water temperatures were only 45 degrees. In the south, these same first movements can be delayed until the water reaches 50 or more degrees. These initial movements demonstrate the intensity of the urge to procreate, and might also serve the purpose of foraging to build reserves for the rigors of the spawn.

As water temperatures rise into the mid-50s, males begin to make nests in gravel, sand, or clay areas. They become very territorial and aggressive during the nest-building process and virtually any fly that passes nearby could be taken. The purpose isn't feeding, but ridding the area of intruders. Nest building can take place on shallow flats with barely enough water to cover the fish's back or, especially in very clear water, in water as deep as 20 feet.

Some have questioned the ethics of fishing for smallmouths during this time of their greatest vulnerability. Years ago, smallmouth bass seasons in many states opened in July. Today, because of the popularity of catch-and-release, we hope, fishing seasons begin earlier. While we have actually observed male smallmouths that we caught from the nest in 55-degree water return to their cleanup work within 10 minutes of release, there are scientific studies that reveal that the guardians may abandon the nests entirely if they are caught after the eggs are laid. When this happens, the eggs and fry are vulnerable to predation. In areas where fishing pressure is light, catching and releasing male nest-guarders might have little effect on spawning success, while post-spawn fishing in heavily fished waters can have a devastating effect on smallmouth numbers.

It's helpful to commit to memory which areas smallmouth bass use for spawning. If, for example, the spawning area is in the back of a cove, pre-spawn staging areas could be an adjacent deeper hump, a rocky secondary point or a brush pile in the middle of the cove. Sometimes when the males are intensely working spawning grounds, the bigger females can be located at one of these staging areas.

The actual spawn can take place as early as the upper 50-degree range and as late as the upper 60's. Feeding during the spawn itself is virtually nonexistent, but fortunately for fishermen, smallmouths are like people in that not all respond to the same stimuli in the same way at the same time. Even during the peak of spawning activity there can be some male fish that are still nest building and some females still in the staging area waiting for their eggs to ripen. There can also be smallmouths of both sexes that have finished the spawning process. These males might be guarding nests and spawned-out females might be back in deeper water recovering from their recent exertion. Still, with the majority of fish participating in the spawn or preparing to do so, feeding activity can be substantially reduced and slow, hit-and-miss fishing action is the result.

While the males are busy parenting, the females wander into deeper water, then scatter. They are nearly impossible to catch during their recuperation process, which may last from a few days to a couple of weeks. Eventually, the scattered females will regroup and move into their summer locations. Males abandon their vulnerable offspring to join the movements to their summer ranges.

Summer for smallmouths occurs when water temperatures reach 70 degrees and lasts until water temperatures rise to their highest levels of the year. This is a time of great abundance for bass as insects, crayfish, minnows, and young-of-the-year fry from all fish species in the lake are available to them. This smorgasbord of feeding opportunities, coupled with migration routes that are complicated by changing weather, makes locating lake smallmouth bass challenging in the summer.

Rocky, mid-lake humps and rock-strewn gravel bars are the choice locations to find summer smallmouths in northern natural lakes. Smallmouth bass use these areas to forage for crayfish and minnows, and in the process they're apt to grab any meal that presents itself. Reservoir bronzebacks use a wider variety of submerged structure including mid-lake humps, gradually sloping points covered with rocks and stumps, riprap areas, piles of dead wood over rock bottoms, submerged concrete foundations, roadbeds, and ledges beneath rock bluffs. They are also attracted to shoals with sparse vegetation where baitfishes are likely to hide. In reservoirs, smallmouths can be found at the mouths of streams where the inflow creates some current and narrow places where wind might produce some current, such as the trough between an island and the shore.

It's possible to locate feeding smallmouths throughout the day, but shallow foraging is most prevalent during periods of low light. Smallmouths often feed in the shallows at night during the summer months especially in southern impoundments that have very clear water and high water temperatures near the surface. As if locating lake smallmouths wasn't challenging enough during the summer, Mother Nature further complicates the process by disrupting their activities with cold fronts. Cold fronts change prevailing weather patterns and usually produce cloud buildups followed by thunderstorms. The problem occurs in the clearing process after the storm is over. A day or more of bright sunny skies, called post-frontal conditions, causes the bass to relocate into deeper water where their visibility is better. Smallmouths sometimes hit during these periods of high sky, but they must be found again as they often move into water that's deep enough to pose problems with both presentation and hook-setting. Perhaps the best solution to the problem of fishing summertime post cold front conditions is fishing under the cover of darkness.

When nights become cooler and the days shorter, the lake's smallmouth population are cued that changes are in order. Because weed growth has reached its peak and prey species are scarcer, the bass are less choosy about their menu. They no longer have the luxury of focusing on their prey of choice and are less apt to ignore your offering. Water levels in most natural lakes and many reservoirs are at their lowest levels. Fish spend longer periods actively pursuing their meals. As water temperatures continue to drop, the intensity and duration of feeding periods increases.

During the early part of autumn, lake smallmouths tend to scatter to feed independently or in small groups of two or three fish. In order to be successful the fly-fisher needs to stay on the move. Success depends on covering lots of water, as opposed to locating a school or casting repeatedly to the same type of structure. Line strips and fly manipulations can be faster at this time when the fish are more inclined to chase their prey for the first time since the aggressive days of spring.

The progression of autumn will cause smallmouth bass to re-group into ever-tightening schools as the water continues to cool. Chasing prey lessens until a slowly stripped fly becomes the only logical retrieve. Smallmouths abandon shallow bars and flats and retreat to progressively deeper structure. By the time water temperatures reach about 50 degrees, fish occupy the deeper portions of their habitat. In natural lakes this location is near the secondary breakline. The same locations and movements apply to impoundments. We've caught smallmouths when water temperatures were as cold as 42 degrees, but it's slow work and unless you're motivated by the satisfaction of locating and catching one or two fish under tough conditions, it becomes a case of too much effort for too little reward. Normally when water temperatures reach 50 degrees in our home lakes, we abandon the big waters and return to the rivers exclusively. See Illustration 4-A for seasonal locations.

Coping With Wind

Wind poses special problems for fly-casters. There are casting techniques and new lines specifically created for windy conditions that facilitate fly-casting when weather isn't cooperative. In addition, the drifting, controlled drifting and trolling techniques described in Chapter 3 can be utilized in many situations. But wind can become dangerous. We've been in situations where white-capping waves have made returning to the launch area real challenges. The larger the lake, the greater the potential for extreme turbulence becomes. The Great Lakes, for example, are very capable of capsizing a boat and turning something done for pleasure into a life-threatening horror story. Some windstorms can arise quickly and unpredictably; therefore, all boat fishermen need to become weather watchers. Ominous looking buildups of clouds and quickening wind conditions need to be heeded. Make sure your vessel is equipped with a motor powerful enough to get you off the water before conditions become dangerous.

Typical Seasonal Locations for Stillwater Smallmouths

First breakline

Secondary breakline

A. *Secondary breakline used in early prespawn as staging area and in fall as a forage area.*

B. *Initial breakline used for late prespawn staging, retreats during cold snaps, postspawn recovering area and in fall as a forage area.*

C. *Gravel flats used as spawning area and in fall as a forage area.*

D. *Mid-lake rock humps or points without weeds used as summer crayfish foraging area.*

E. *Mid-lake humps or points with weed crown used as summer minnow foraging area.*

F. *Wintering locations in still waters that freeze over. Fish are in neutral or negative feeding mood.*

Illustration 4-A

Stillwater provides a somewhat easier lifestyle for smallmouth bass than moving water.

Stillwater provides a somewhat easier lifestyle for smallmouth bass than moving water. They don't need to burn excessive calories to maintain themselves or their positions in the water and there's a wide variety of readily available prey species. The result is that lake smallmouths tend to become larger than their current-bound relatives, but for a variety of reasons, lake fishing by fly-fishers is largely ignored in many parts of the country. While it's an entirely different game of location and presentation, it offers smallmouth fly-fishing aficionados a new frontier to explore and the possibility of catching the fish of a lifetime.

Seven- and 8-weight outfits are best on lakes because the increased size of the available food forms translate into larger, heavier, and sometimes more wind-resistant flies. Many lakes that have smallmouth populations host only isolated pockets of the species. They are rarely the dominant species whether the water is a natural northern lake or a mid-South reservoir. Fishing efforts should be concentrated around classic elements of structure. Rarely will a pile of rocks among many piles of rocks be the most productive. The structure that holds the most and best fish will be the biggest rock pile of the most diverse sizes with access to both shallow, graveled flats and relatively deep water nearby.

Fly Color In Stillwater

As traditionalists, our stillwater flies were originally tied in more natural hues, thus browns, olives, and tans tended to dominate our fly selections. More recently we've joined other smallmouth bass anglers in experimenting with some wild colors. Fluorescent chartreuse, orange, and pink have been given good testings. We believe that colors appear differently to smallmouths under changing light and water conditions. To our surprise, a crayfish fly tied in chartreuse is perfectly acceptable, even preferred at times, by our smallmouths. We've also cast gaudy orange over chartreuse streamers that have worked well.

Fly color isn't a critical factor in triggering strikes in deep water because colors tend to become an indistinct shade of gray in water deeper than 15 feet. For our deep-water fishing, we use predominantly black flies to produce sharp silhouettes.

With the exception of extremely deep water, say in excess of 20 feet, the fly-fisher has several advantages. First, when the bass are shallow, the splashdown of our flies is much less likely to disturb the fish. Second, we can fish our offering through a productive area, then pick up and cast again to another productive area without having to bring the offering through water likely to be devoid of fish. And finally, our flies have likely not been seen by these lake-dwelling bass that long ago became so accustomed to plugs that they could identify them by model numbers.

CHAPTER 5
MOVING WATER

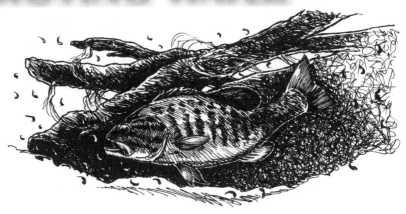

I t's easy to fall in love with rivers. They awaken our sens-
es, invigorate our minds, and provide inspiration to our
souls. As children of the Illinois prairies, we came to appreciate the incomparable beauty of rivers later than most.
In retrospect that seems odd because we were reared within
minutes of the majestic Mississippi. It commanded attention,
to be sure, but its muddy flow interrupted by massive hydro-
electric dams failed to inspire yearnings to wander along its
shallows or to discover the charms concealed by the next bend
in the river. Road trips in the 1950's to visit the Wilson clan in
neighboring Missouri were often interrupted by wading and
swimming breaks to seek relief from the heat of mid-summer
afternoons. Terry's journeys of discovery spawned a lifelong
fascination with the therapeutic pulse of moving water.

How strange it seemed to him to stand in waist-deep water
while viewing his own bare feet. Swimming under water with
open eyes enabled a fish's view of life beneath the surface. Bot-
tom-dwelling crayfish were clearly visible and pursued with
exuberance before the distraction of butterflies hovering over

bankside wildflowers became the next source of wonder. Frogs were chased across gravel bars, herons were flushed from hidden pools, and streambanks were scoured for flat little stones to achieve multiple hops in rock-skipping competitions. These "cricks" had a pleasant, earthy smell that lingered long after his return to the flatlands and rekindled memories of his adventures. Eventually, the focus of his river trips came to rest upon the smallmouth bass that inhabited these magical waterways as the peaceful rhythms of these sanctuaries powerfully beckoned him to return.

Fly-fishing for smallmouth bass in moving water provides trout fanciers who want to expand their horizons with a relatively undemanding transition into warmwater fly-fishing. The equipment requirements are so similar that there are virtually no additional expenses. Most trout anglers are already familiar with reading the water and will therefore understand many of the smallmouth's locational preferences and the flies that are applicable to both species. Stream fishing for smallmouths offers a substantial upside. The nation's public trout streams, as well as many warmwater lakes, are awash with anglers while many smallmouth bass rivers are relatively free of competition. Lots of streams, even some near major cities, offer plenty of solitude as naturally reproducing smallmouth populations defy neglect and prosper.

Smallmouth streams come in many sizes, from trickling brooks anglers can step across to major navigable rivers. There are thousands of miles of moving water that harbor smallmouths, but an equally large number of miles that do not. Since smallmouth bass are a very adaptable species it's difficult to establish even wide parameters of water characteristics in which the fish can survive. We've encountered healthy populations in some warm streams where summer water surface temperatures exceed 90 degrees. We have found them in sections of rivers where water levels fluctuated dramatically and from waters that appear too turbid. Competing species, such as largemouth bass, crappie, walleye, and northern pike, may be the only limiting factor as to where smallmouths are capable of residing.

It's a lot easier to define which river characteristics are preferred by smallmouths. Generally, waterways that come closest to these ideals have the largest self-sustaining populations of smallmouth bass. That's really the quality fishery that interests anglers anyway. The only reason to fish a marginal population of smallmouths comes about when nearby streams offer short, but decent, sections of catch-and-release fishing.

Nearly all good smallmouth rivers contain lots of rocks. Diversity of rock size can make a good smallmouth stream into a great one or contribute a great section to otherwise lackluster water. Rocks are important for several reasons. They provide hiding and feeding positions for crayfish, which rank as the number one food source for stream smallmouths. State fisheries biologists tell us that as much as 80 percent of the stream smallmouth's diet is crayfish in the warmer months. Abundant rocks, whether in the form of manmade riprap areas or chunk rocks of similar size, provide foraging places for the bass.

High-quality smallmouth water also contains some scattered rocks. Rocks of several feet in diameter up to the size of a small pickup truck provide shade, cover, and current breaks for the fish. In addition, prime smallmouth habitat is constituted of large, relatively shallow areas of gravel or sand that allow for successful reproduction.

Ideally, the smallmouth spends most of its days sheltered from the incessant current while feeding opportunistically on any of a wide variety of food items that may present themselves. The bass may make several foraging trips each day to actively search for food. Often, the trips take them to the riffle at the head of a pool, and sometimes, especially under low light conditions, they go to graveled shallows near the stream banks. Smallmouths feed at the pool's tailout if there are current breaks. A tailout is an area of quickening water above a riffle at the downstream end of a pool. In this area, current draws food to the bass before the morsels are swept into the next pool. These tailout areas are usually best in the evening. Just as a relatively small percentage of habitats hold smallmouths in lakes, so only the very best or rockiest areas are magnets for them in rivers. Stretches of streams where rocky environments smooth to flat, graveled or sandy areas may be devoid of smallmouth bass most of the time.

Smallmouths prefer streams that are comprised of riffles, deeper pools, and tailout areas that lead to other pools downstream. This riffle-pool-riffle arrangement provides a well-oxygenated environment that offers shallow foraging areas as well as deep-water retreats. It also provides a healthy atmosphere for a variety of insect species, the favored crayfish, and a wide variety of minnow inhabitants with weedy, shaded banks that hold frogs and terrestrials.

Despite the existence of healthy, active smallmouths in tepid streams in southeastern Oklahoma, most smallmouths are found in spring-fed streams with summer water temperatures between 70 and 85 degrees. Smallmouths also prefer clean, well oxygenated, but nutrient-enriched water. Generally, bass in warm waters will remain active and catchable as long as shade covers preferred structure. Southeast Oklahoma guide, Rob Woodruff, advises, "Fish early and late in the day in hot water and avoid casting to sunlit areas. Shade is the key to finding active smallmouths in extremely warm water."

Current speed is another factor that affects the smallmouth's basic needs. Water that's too swift makes the fish's energy expenditure too great to allow survival, while waters that are too slow are more conducive to largemouth bass and less inviting for smallmouth bass. Current speed is determined by how greatly the streambed drops in elevation each mile along its course, which is termed its gradient. Gradients of approximately 4 feet per mile are necessary to produce a ripple and pool arrangement. Streams with a gradient in excess of 7 feet per mile are about the upper limit of preferred smallmouth bass habitat. Obviously, a trained eye is necessary to estimate stream gradient on sight, but if the river has well defined riffles at the heads of the pools, pools, and tailouts it will fit those criteria. Of course, when our hypothetical stream floods or when drought prevents the riffles from running, the smallmouth bass must struggle to survive. Streams that suffer the least extremes in water levels and flow, except in rare cases, will provide the best smallmouth fishing.

Reading Rivers

The amount of water flowing in the river, its overall size, including width and depth, as well as its gradient all help to determine its current speed. A 3-inch downpour causes additional water to enter the river and increases the speed of its current. When a wide, flat stretch of river narrows between canyon walls more water is forced through the smaller section thus the current becomes faster. Current speed changes not only within the same stream but also within the same pool. Often we cast from a stationary position into the current but fail to recognize that returning our flies to the same spot that was productive before the rain doesn't take into account that the flies will not sink, drift or swim in the same way because the current has quickened.

Many seasons ago we were camped on an isolated stretch of a classic smallmouth stream. Every evening for a week we entered the water at a tailout and cast streamers upriver where we retrieved them alongside a piano-sized boulder. We caught fish after fish there, and we christened the place "the evening pool." One morning a gentle rain fell and when we returned after supper we found the river a couple of inches higher. Now our upstream casts tumbled downstream too quickly and didn't get deep enough to interest a single smallmouth. It didn't take much of a change in conditions to totally alter our success. Understanding how currents react to the contour of the stream bottom allows the fly-fisher to recognize where smallmouths are able to locate. The water's surface will provide clues about what's found beneath, and "reading" and interpreting these visual signs enables the angler to cast to areas for a drift or retrieve through the most productive water.

Obstructions, such as large rocks, that slow the current provide an opportunity for smallmouths to rest and feed. Smallmouths locate either immediately in front of or behind the obstruction. The water's surface will show a hump or bulge of water just downstream from the obstruction because the stream's flow is interrupted and doesn't have the same force as nearby unobstructed water. As a result, fish expend much less energy to maintain their positions. Cast upstream of the bulge to allow the offering to drift and drop deeply enough that the fish can see it as it passes overhead or is swept past the structure. One simple means of recognizing the smallmouths' potential hangouts is understanding structures that serve as obstructions to the stream's flow. Here are some of the structures that are easily recognized and a few examples of the flies and tactics that might be applied with each.

A shallow gravel bar interspersed with larger chunk rock that is located on the inside bend of a river provides a smallmouth hangout. A riffle that flows across the bar into relatively deep water provides a clue that bass might be feeding downstream from the riffle. Generally these places are gentle flows that bring oxygen and food to the waiting bass population. Hatches of insects might occur in these areas and, in the absence of duns rising from the surface, it's a good place to fish smaller nymphs. Chubs and other small fish may gather to feed below these riffles so streamers can be productive here as well.

Downed trees, log jams, root wads, or abandoned beaver lodges might hold bass on their downstream sides or immediately upstream. Such structure can be viewed if part of it juts above the water line or by noting its telltale bulge on the water's surface. These large current breaks provide overhead cover, shade, and oxygenated water. Bass utilize the area as a feeding station by lying in the reduced flow and watching for morsels of food to be swept toward their position. Larger nymphs and

Large rocks that slow the current give smallmouths the opportunity to rest and feed.

minnow imitations are effective. Many times smallmouths in these situations will refuse a small offering but move out into the current swiftly to grab a substantial meal.

Riprap that has been placed at the bases of bridge supports and riprap areas that protrude into the water to prevent erosion should be cast to as well. Islands, humps, and depressions, all common smallmouth haunts, also change the intensity of the current. Weighted crayfish imitations dead-drifted with sporadic twitches that activate the imitation can be lethal in these areas. Match-the-minnow imitations and marabou streamers can also be productive.

Wing dams are sometimes constructed on large rivers. They are built in navigable rivers to divert the current's flow away from shore and into the main channel. Manmade wing dams provide downstream current breaks and eddies. An eddy is a side pool where the water swirls away from the downstream current flow. These variations in current are usually very slow, easily spotted, and easily fished. If the bottom content is suitable, eddies can be used as spawning areas. Most often the outside edges of slow-moving whirlpools are the best locations for fish because the reverse current sweeps food to them. The upstream side or face of wing dams should also be explored. Heavily weighted Clousers or crayfish flies are often successful when cast in close proximity to the face of the wing dam and retrieved parallel to it. The area behind and immediately downstream from this major current break can be a bass magnet as well. If the smallmouths are particularly active they will position themselves just inside the end of the wing dam near the point of increased current. They often lie parallel to the wing dam so that food swept by in the eddy can be seen if they are aggressively feeding. Bass with a neutral feeding attitude are likely to locate nearer the center of the eddy where foam builds up. Eddies can be important targets in locating river smallmouths. As with all structure patterns, it's important to identify the location of productive eddies, and equally important to identify which parts of the eddies are serving up hits.

In addition to wing dams, many elements of structure cause eddies. Gravel bars, piles of woody debris, and bottom or shore bound deadfalls divert water resulting in an eddy. By noticing the material that causes the eddy, as well as its depth, size, and shape, fly-fishers can select their flies accordingly and place them in the best positions to trigger hits. Two examples are shallow eddies with gravel bottoms that are preferred areas for crayfish and eddies created by deadfalls that often harbor small schools of minnows.

Aquatic vegetation also serves as current breaks and as filters when the water carries silt from recent rains. The downstream side of a weedbed is not only a good smallmouth location because of reduced current, but during periods of dirty water it may be slightly clearer so the fish are better able to see their prey. If the current is relatively gentle and dragonflies, damselflies or dobsonflies are present, this situation presents an opportunity to drift nymphs or hellgrammite patterns adjacent to the weeds.

Undercut banks also provide good hiding places for smallmouths out of the current. Food often washes past their lairs and they can opportunistically dart out to grab it. Depending on the attending cover, these areas can be difficult to fish. It's important to cast slack line well above the undercut bank and permit the current to sweep your offering into the fish's vision. If rocks are part of the picture, crayfish imitations can bring solid strikes. If the location is shaded and appears deep and dark we like dark-colored flies in black, olive, and purple. Large woolly buggers can be a good choice.

Feeder streams, especially those that are spring fed and occur in concert with any of the aforementioned structural elements can be the summer and winter homes of large numbers of smallmouths. Spring creeks enter at constant temperatures, cooling the water in summer and warming it in winter. If the spring-fed feeder stream is large enough, smallmouths are likely to use it extensively during times of extreme heat or cold. Current breaks in feeder streams need to be evaluated and fished in the same manner as the main river. It should be noted that feeder streams are generally shallower than the rivers they feed and may receive less fishing pressure. If the main source of the feeder stream's flow is one or more springs it may also be considerably clearer. These circumstances dictate a stealthier approach, a finer leader, and possibly lighter- colored flies and floating line. Since all of these changes in tackle options are relative they must be evaluated on a case-by-case basis.

Bluff areas that provide shade over relatively deep, rock-infested water can also provide for the needs of many smallmouths when they seek refuge from heat or cold. Most bluffs overlook relatively deep, slow pools. Sink-tip or even full-sinking lines may be needed to probe the depths with weighted flies. Yet if overhanging brush or rockslides have created shallow cover a popper or floater/diver on floating line might be the best option. Each end of the bluff may be an exceptional smallmouth location and should command additional attention. See Illustration 5-A to view smallmouth locations in a typical river with diverse structural elements.

One of the most productive locations that hold large smallmouths is the slow-flowing area near shore in slack water near the point at which the current begins to accelerate toward the tailout of a pool. Even if this area has no other elements of structure, the bigger fish find living there easy. A few casts there before moving on to the next pool can hook the best fish of the day.

Another productive area found in many pools is the point at which slower current meets faster current. This situation creates a visible line or "seam" on the water's surface. Smallmouths often lie in the slower current and watch for food drifting along in the swifter water. By utilizing a down-and-across presentation in combination with a reach cast, the angler can drift or manipulate the fly right along the seam where bass are poised to strike. Nymphs and minnow imitators are particularly productive in seams, as are vertical drop flies with wiggly parts that activate in the crosscurrents.

It's important to calculate how rapidly flies sink at different current speeds. It does no good to understand where bass are located if we simply float our imitations too far above them or our flies are swept away from targets by cross currents that we hadn't taken into account. The speed of the current and the depth of the water determine which flies, lines, and even leader

Typical Smallmouth Holding Areas in Moving Water

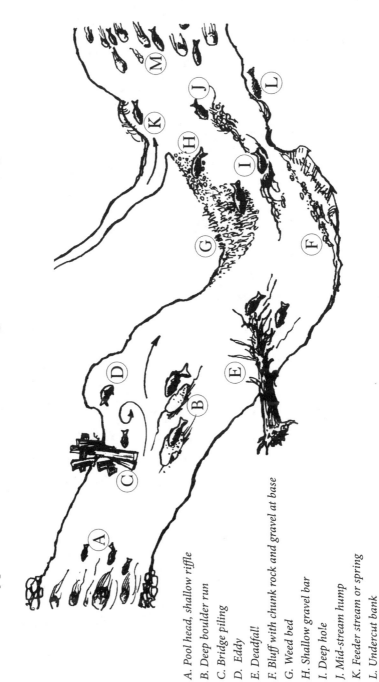

A. Pool head, shallow riffle
B. Deep boulder run
C. Bridge piling
D. Eddy
E. Deadfall
F. Bluff with chunk rock and gravel at base
G. Weed bed
H. Shallow gravel bar
I. Deep hole
J. Mid-stream hump
K. Feeder stream or spring
L. Undercut bank
M. Pool tail-out

Illustration 5-A

Large current breaks such as rootwads provide cover, shade, and oxygenated water.

selections are necessary for the targeted area. One of our favorite stretches of pocket water near home best illustrates this point. Pocket water is flowing water that's interrupted by many large rocks in its path. This particular section of river looks bumpy due to the bulges created on its surface as water flows over submerged rocks. If this water were 3 to 6 feet deep with a moderate current, an unweighted fly on floating fly line would have little chance to get into the fish zone. Conversely, if the

Smallmouth bass streams are often the most scenic in the region.

SHALLOW WATER FLIES

Huffman's Hexagenia
tied by Mike Huffman

Allen Lite Popper
tied by Dave Whitlock

**Most Whit Hair Bug
(Fruit Cocktail)**
tied by Dave Whitlock

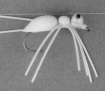

**Dave's
Sponge Spider**
tied by Dave Whitlock

Modified Sofa Pillow
tied by Terry Wilson

**Huffman's
Mud Dauber**
tied by Mike Huffman

SHALLOW WATER FLIES

Murphy's Western Hopper
tied by Jim Murphy

Joe's Sponge Spider
tied by Joe Amoinette

Whitlock's Diving Frog (modified)
tied by Mike Huffman

**Dave's Orange Belly
Diving Frog**
tied by Dave Whitlock

**Wilson's
Hula Diver**
tied by Terry Wilson

MID-DEPTH FLIES

North Fork Nymph
tied by Terry Wilson

Bead Body Bass Buster tied by John Henry

Rob's Krystal Bugger
tied by Rob Woodruff

Marabou Black-Nosed Dace
tied by Doug Farthing

Marc's Magic Minnow
tied by Marc Pinsel

Squirrel-Spin 2K
tied by Terry Wilson

Tanner's Kraft-Hair Minnow
tied by Terry Tanner

MID-DEPTH FLIES (cont'd)

Wilson's Lil' Shad
tied by Terry Wilson

Drop Nose Minnow
tied by Dave Duffy

Murray's Strymph
tied by Dave Duffy

Meiler's Pine Squirrel Leech
tied by Elmer Meiler

Rob's W.I.T.H. Bugger
tied by Rob Woodruff

Terry's New Guinea Bugger
tied by Terry Tanner

Bead Head Peacock Woolly Bugger
tied by Terry Wilson

BOTTOM/DEEPWATER FLIES

Dave's Nearnuff Sculpin
tied by Dave Whitlock

Hada's Madtom
tied by Duane Hada

Verduin's Hellgrammite
tied by Michael Verduin

**Verduin's
Dragonfly Nymph**
tied by Michael Verduin

**Farthing's Mottled
Stonefly Nymph**
tied by Doug Farthing

**Whitlock's Bead Chain
Sili Leg Red Fox Squirrel Nymph**
tied by Dave Whitlock

BOTTOM/DEEPWATER FLIES (cont'd)

Wilson's Bass Bully
tied by Terry Wilson

Whitlock's Scorpion Fly
tied by Dave Whitlock

CRAYFISH FLIES

Christian's Jig Crayfish
tied by Doug Christian

Hada's Creek Crawler
tied by Duane Hada

Schmuecker's Pine Craw
tied by Joe Schmuecker

The Fritz Pine Craw
tied by Steve Fritz

CRAYFISH FLIES (cont'd)

The Rusty Sparrow (modified) tied by Kyle Moppert

Whitlock's Nearnuff Crayfish tied by Dave Whitlock

Tanner's Crawdad tied by Terry Tanner

Crawman tied by Dave Duffy

Halblom's Crayfish tied by David Halblom

Rivers invigorate our minds and provide inspiration to our souls.

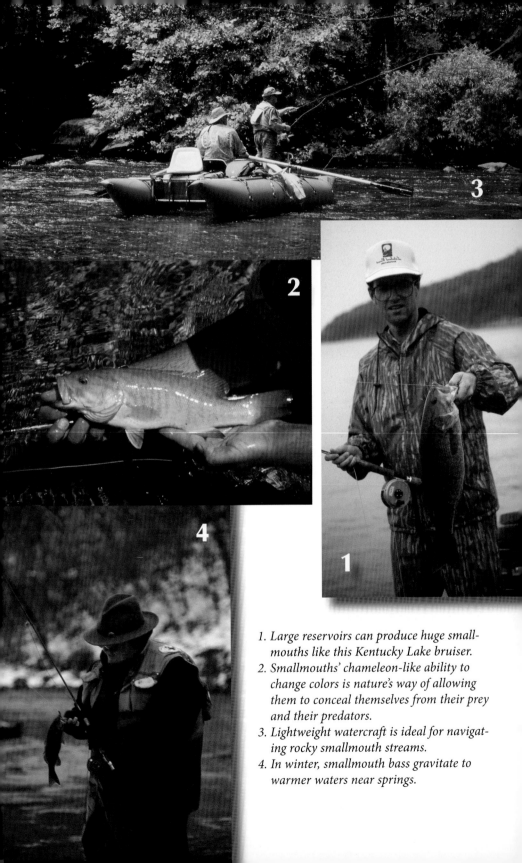

1. *Large reservoirs can produce huge small-mouths like this Kentucky Lake bruiser.*
2. *Smallmouths' chameleon-like ability to change colors is nature's way of allowing them to conceal themselves from their prey and their predators.*
3. *Lightweight watercraft is ideal for navigating rocky smallmouth streams.*
4. *In winter, smallmouth bass gravitate to warmer waters near springs.*

5. *The quiet pools of autumn offer some of the year's best fishing.*

6. *Sunrise in summer is an ideal time to enjoy rivers and small-mouth bass fishing.*

7. *An undercut bank that offers shade and protection is an excellent smallmouth bass location.*

8

9

10

8. The best approach to prospecting for riverine bronzebacks is beaching the canoe and wading upstream and down.
9. Smallmouths take advantage of current breaks in fast water. Look for eddies and surface bulges caused by large rocks.
10. A gravel bar with chunk rock on the inside bend of a river can be a small-mouth hangout.

depth of the pocket water were 2 feet and the current sluggish, a lead-laced fly on sinking line could hang up on the rocky bottom constantly. A weighted fly on a 6-foot leader using sink-tip line allows an appropriate presentation for the moderate current and 3- to 6-foot depths. To accomplish the same drift in shallow, sluggish current a slightly weighted fly, 9-foot leader, and floating line would be needed.

The scientific studies we've read, the guides we've consulted, and our own fishing experiences have led us to speculate that each population of smallmouths that is confined to a particular river system might well have developed behaviors and movements that don't match those of smallmouth bass in other waterways. In spite of the confusion about river smallmouth movement, anglers have been successful in catching them in a widely different set of geographic locations and climates. The reason for it is that, despite unpredictable fish movements, recognizing and effectively presenting flies to the use areas we've previously described is universal. It is helpful to recognize whether there exists an adequate spawning and rearing site within the confines of a particular pool, and, if there is not, where the nearest spawning area is located. Identifying the deep-water safe havens that the bass can use is also important. If anglers, other predators or an impending storm put them on alert, smallmouths tend to seek the security of relatively deep waters. When they're located in their safe lies they usually have negative, or at least neutral, feeding attitudes. The chances of catching them in this situation are not particularly high, but it helps us understand the smallmouths' movements so we can predict where they might go to resume foraging when the coast is clear.

Rivers are never static. Sometimes they change radically, at other times, imperceptibly. The most radical overnight change is runoff due to rains or snowmelt, which rather suddenly overwhelm the river with an increased volume of water. With the rising waters, the once-placid stream becomes a raging torrent that carries silt and debris. As the stream falls back within its banks and conditions improve, the fly-caster can return, but fishing the same areas that were successful before the deluge will get him skunked quicker than a politician's handshake.

High, stained water forces the fish to stick very close to major current breaks, gravitate to the protected shallows or seek refuge in the mouths of feeder streams. Although little waterways will carry dirty water, too, they rise more quickly but fall faster than the main river. Bass enter these creeks and swim some distance upstream to find conditions that are more suitable for foraging. In our experience, flood conditions actually make locating smallmouths easier because the fish are concentrated. Dingy water makes it more difficult for them to see their food, but it also provides security that's lacking in clear water. Fly-fishers can take advantage of the situation by using flies that create a disturbance. A popper can do the job if it's fished in the slack water behind major current breaks or among weeds and grass near shore. Flies designed to utilize rattles, twister tails, or small spinners will attract fish that plainly dressed flies won't. Our most successful flies when fishing high, roily water are those with barbell eyes such as Clousers. Lead barbell eyes allow us to use the rock-banging technique described in Chapter 3. Clicking noises from banging the fly into rocky current breaks triggers the bass's strikes. Floods dislocate aquatic and terrestrial insects, too. Big stonefly nymphs, hexagenia nymphs, and hellgrammites, fished very slowly, can fetch smallmouths from high water

In clear water conditions it's difficult to approach larger fish in the shallows. Double-hauled casts with sparsely tied flies and long, fine leaders must be accompanied by stealthy approaches. Muddy water changes the tactics. Anglers can get within just a few feet of fish-holding structure with casts of 15 to 20 feet. Using shorter, stronger leaders is best. Repeated casts to the same current break may be necessary. If the break is a large rock, the area should be thoroughly covered from different angles before moving on. Even after catching several bass, don't abandon the area too quickly. The number of good holding areas under muddy conditions is relatively low, but it's possible that several fish have located behind the current break.

Just as ultra-clear water requires sparsely tied flies, dirty water situations are best confronted with heavily dressed flies. The stronger the silhouette, the more likely it is that the smallmouths will see it. Also, bulky flies displace more water, which causes more sound to be transmitted.

It seems that every streamside philosopher has a different opinion when it comes to fly color. Some suggest that lighter-colored flies, such as white, silver, yellow, and chartreuse, reflect more light, which is necessary so that more fish can see the flies. Others prefer darker colors, such as purple and black, to create strong outlines for the fish to see against the lighter-colored sky as they view the flies from below. Both opinions are valid in our judgment, and whichever is best depends in general on the darkness of the water. In clear or slightly stained water we prefer reflective colors. Flies tied in white/silver, yellow/gold or chartreuse produce best for us. In downright muddy water we stick to large, bulky black flies.

Water clarity, except in extreme cases, should be evaluated on the basis of what is considered normal for that particular stream. Clear conditions generally mean clearer than normal, while stained implies darker water than is usually the case. In streams that are usually clear, their cloudiest appearance might be clearer than a normal flow on a nearby stream where cloudy might be considered the norm. The fishing application is that clear-water smallmouths are accustomed to sight feeding and will take bulkier and darker flies when their streams are murky. On normally murky streams that are low and clearer, sparsely tied flies in subtle colors may be more productive.

When the Water Is Low and Clear

In the absence of abundant rains as the season moves into late summer or autumn the volume of water carried by rivers becomes less. Even spring-fed streams receive less groundwater so their volume is reduced. As the stream turns shallower and clearer, its character changes. Springs and feeder creeks may be at their lowest ebb; some pools in smaller waterways may cease to flow at all. It's sometimes possible to observe the bass but equally possible for them to see you. Approaching fish in this situation can be extremely difficult but employing the stealth of a turkey or deer hunter is a good start.

Paying attention to each detail of the fishing strategy yields excellent dividends. Stealth will enable approaches to points within casting distance. Still, casts will need to be longer and leaders lengthened with finer tippets to prevent spooking the fish. If the trip has evolved into a sight-fishing exercise, don't focus entirely on selected smallmouths. Spooking nearby bluegills and other sunfish alert these cautious fish to the angler's presence even though they've not seen or heard the intrusions themselves.

Smallmouths tend to be tightly bunched in low, clear water and any strike, whether successful or not, may put every fish in the pool on red alert. It's important to keep moving and cover a lot of territory with gentle casts and subtle flies. Noisemakers are a hindrance here. Select smaller, more sparsely dressed flies and avoid those with spinners, twister tails, and rattles. Dead-drifting a nymph or crawling a tiny crayfish may be necessary to pique the bass's interest. The fly-fisher's dilemma is that smaller flies may be taken by one of the sunfish in the pool and the resulting disturbance may put the smallmouths down. Under these extreme conditions, the only option available may have bad, but unavoidable, results.

Since smallmouths can see remarkably well in clear water and they are accustomed to feeding by sight, they are able to carefully scrutinize our imposters. If ever an angler were inclined to use realistic imitations, these conditions would warrant it. Matching the hatch, the minnow, and the crayfish with regard to size, appearance, action, and color are reasonable considerations.

Clearwater smallmouth fly boxes contain brown, tan, shades of olive, and gray creations tied in smaller sizes. Many incorporate materials such as marabou, rabbit, or pine squirrel for lifelike action. Flies should be dead-drifted, then gently twitched at intervals. Rather than making repeated casts to the same area, it's important to fan-cast the pool and return to the same feeding lane only after it's rested for a few minutes.

While the water is usually very clear during droughts, it often has a greater than normal amount of suspended particles and a thin layer of silt and algae on the bottom. Oxygen is reduced in shallow areas as the water warms so the smallmouths seek the comfort of deep holes, especially those with springs, and locate below riffles to feed. Insect patterns in bigger sizes that are fished slowly will produce hits. Adult damselfly and grasshopper patterns work well if the drought occurs in mid-summer. Keep in mind that severe drought affects the numbers and availability of insects not only in the present, but in future seasons, and can affect the productivity of some insect patterns after water levels return to normal. Fish caught from too warm, poorly oxygenated water can be stressed beyond the point of recovery and should be played and released as quickly as possible.

Matching Crayfish Fly Color To Stream Clarity

In the mid-'90's, while camped beside a very clear stream, we observed smallmouths actually fleeing from our crayfish offerings. True enough, the sunlight penetration was intense, but we hardly expected that reaction to our best flies. Returning to camp, we unpacked a vise and attempted to match the subtle coloration of the naturals we had observed. Eventually, we settled on a sparsely tied, tan-colored pattern that utilized marabou as the tail and tan ostrich herl as the body which covered 20 turns of .020 lead wire. The flies weren't terribly durable, but we spent five memorable evenings around the campfire reliving the acrobatic fight of an enormous number of eager bronzebacks.

Strangely, when we fished the same flies in our more stained home waters, our success took a direct hit. Similarly tied olive creations, however, took up the slack. After several trips back and forth between the two rivers, we realized that flies fished as crayfish needed a coloration consistent with the bottom content of the stream in order to be effective. To generalize, olive crayfish patterns are most effective in streams that are off color or murky with dark bottoms. Light tan-colored crayfish patterns are far more effective in very clear water where there are light-colored bottoms. As Arkansas guide Duane Hada reminds us, "If you have trouble seeing your crayfish patterns against the background of the bottom, its color is just right."

Weather changes, including fronts that change the atmospheric pressure, don't have the same radically negative impact upon river fishing that they have in still water. The current tends to nullify the effect of the atmospheric pressure.

Because life is more difficult in moving water, which causes fish to work harder to survive, the bass are more willing to feed for longer periods of time. We've done well in streams at midday during the warmest days of the year with sunlight overhead seeming to cast spotlights into the water. On a recent float trip we slowly drifted past 14- to 16-inch smallmouths cruising over a mid-stream light-colored bottom. We landed two that were colored a very pale, mottled tan. Within the same pool we caught another smallmouth that was coaxed from an undercut bank. This fish was a rich brown/olive in color with the smallmouth's signature iridescent bronze sheen. These fish looked very different from one another, yet they were from the same gene pool and perhaps the same year class. The chameleon-like ability to change colors is nature's way of allowing smallmouths to conceal themselves from their prey and their predators.

As we passed over these sunlit pools, we could not see crayfish. The bright conditions had apparently driven them into crevices in the rocks for safety and comfort. The open water bass rejected our crayfish offerings, but fell victim to minnow imitations. The fish that came from the undercut bank hit a crayfish pattern on the first drift.

Understanding the effects of current and reading the changing conditions of moving water will enable you to catch and release more big smallmouth bass. Analyzing each situation in which fish were encountered will enable you to repeat your successes on subsequent angling excursions.

CHAPTER 6
SHALLOW WATER TACTICS AND FLIES

C atching smallmouth bass on the surface surely has to rank as one of life's most delectable pleasures. Whether the imitation is sipped delicately or taken with a flash of bronze and a shower of quicksilver, the experience often elicits an audible laugh of delight even when fishing in solitude. If it's not the very essence of the sport of fly-fishing, it comes very close. Fortunately, the possibility of this visually stimulating game can be a regular occurrence from the time the water begins to warm in spring until at least mid-autumn, and it can be the most effective method of fishing under a variety of circumstances. Visual clues tell the angler when it will be a viable presentation.

Before entering the river or while cruising into a promising cove in stillwater, an observant angler is likely to notice the telltale signs of surface potential. If there is a heavy insect hatch and regular rises of feeding fish, noisy splashes, swirls on the surface or minnows spraying wildly from unseen predators, topwater fishing may be the order of the day.

Dry Flies

In the spring when caddisfly and mayfly hatches are most abundant and crayfish of edible size are less so, dry flies can be most effective. Matching the hatch can certainly be productive, but seeing the hatch and replicating its color and size are not guarantees that the smallmouths will respond. Often we've spotted a significant hatch and seen but a few smallmouth rises or only little fish pursuing them. This seems to be especially true when other, much larger preferred prey is abundant. Spring is normally a time when rivers are high and off color, which can eliminate the best dry fly action, but we always carry our dry flies anyway and welcome the opportunity to use them.

Each river system has its own hatches that must be matched accordingly, but smallmouths are generally less demanding about matching hatches than trout. While tying to match a specific hatch can provide its own rewards, we've been successful with more impressionistic patterns.

To simulate caddisfly hatches, Elk Hair Caddis are a reasonable choice that's readily available from fly shops. Mayfly hatches are abundant on rivers in much of the smallmouth's range. If it is a plentiful hatch, they can turn on a whole pool of bass.

Fishing a hatch of large mayfly duns is often a bit different from trout fishing under the same circumstance. Targeting slower water a bit downstream from the fast flow is the rule rather than the exception because bass don't always stay in feeding lanes and rise regularly as is expected in classic dry-fly trout fishing. Instead, smallmouths sometimes cruise the pool while attempting to grab as many duns as possible. If the fish's movements are visible, its speed and direction can be anticipated so the fly can be dropped in its path. If the fish can't be seen, casting blindly and getting the best drift possible often works, but toward the end of the drift try quivering the fly by shaking the rod tip. This tactic often interests reluctant fish. Most fly shops carry a wide selection of mayfly patterns.

When giant Hexagenias are hatching, one of the best imitations is Huffman's Hexagenia. Mike Huffman, a very talented tyer and fly designer, offers his creative pattern.

Huffman's Hexagenia

Hook: Dai-Riki #135, size 6 or heavy wire scud hook, size 8
Tail: Wood duck flank, 3 fibers for each fork married using flexible cement
Abdomen and Thorax: Yellow 1/8-inch sheet foam (piece cut 1 ½ inches long, 3/8 inch wide tapered to 1/8 inch wide for abdomen)
Wing: Bleached elk hair, dyed yellow
Color: Fine point brown permanent marker, if desired
Cement: Super Glue
Tying Instructions:
Abdomen assembly: Use a large sewing needle in the vise with the point forward to assemble abdomen. Define the 8 segments of the foam abdomen. Spiral the thread back to the tail in crisscross fashion. Carefully slide the assembly off the needle. Do not cut off the remaining foam.
Body: Mount the hook in the vise point up. Tie in the abdomen assembly with a 1/8-inch wide collar of wraps so that a ½-inch flap extends forward. To form the thorax, pinch the abdomen flap in an inverted "U" and back it up ¼ inch to create the hump of the thorax. Add segment and thorax markings with a marker.

While smallmouths may not insist on exact duplication, they are casting critics. Sloppy casting and presentation will relegate even perfect patterns to arrogant refusals.

With nearly four hundred species of stoneflies in North America, it's not surprising that they come in a variety of sizes. Some are as small as 1/8 inch long while others exceed 2 inches with 4-inch wingspans. Larger stoneflies can spend up to 2 years in their nymphal stage before crawling out of the water to rest on rocks, trees or bushes at the water's edge while they allow their wings to dry. Although various species of stoneflies hatch year around, the greatest numbers are available to smallmouths in spring. In the western Untied States, large adult stoneflies, known as salmon flies, are worthy of imitation because small-mouths feed ravenously on them when they're available. Again, impressionistic patterns will suffice. As Arkansas guide Duane Hada told us, "Don't fool smallmouths. Just feed them." In terms of fishing success, matching the general size and floatability of adult stoneflies seems more important than specific patterns.

Poppers, Sliders, and Wakers

Poppers are the most popular fly choice for topwater bass. They float on or in the surface so that they can be manipulated to make audible disturbances to imitate the floundering, desperate struggles of unlucky creatures that have fallen into the water or the erratic movements of frogs and injured minnows. Without question, poppers can trigger some heart-thumping strikes.

Poppers are made of cork, closed-cell foam, balsa or spun deer hair. They're widely available and configured in a variety of colors and sizes to represent frogs, wounded minnows, and even large moths. The appropriate popper sizes aren't immune from frequent attacks by small panfish. Green sunfish have relatively large mouths, but even the beautifully colored longear sunfish and bluegills are aggressive enough to take their best shots at your smallmouth poppers. Such interference can be a nuisance, of course, but it does have an upside. Several times each season we've had big smallmouths grab the struggling pan-fish we were retrieving. If you can strip loose coils of line from your reel fast enough and shake the rod tip to deposit the loose coils of line on the water so that the greedy bass doesn't feel any pressure, you actually have a fair chance of landing both fish without a hook penetrating the smallmouth. The trick is to let the bass have the sunfish long enough that it is reluctant to let go. In our experience the time this requires is between 30 seconds and a minute. At that point exerting even, steady pressure can bring the fish to hand. Some of these "hookless" hookups will result in the bass simply releasing its catch, but numerous times in the past few seasons we have been able to land and subsequently release both fish.

Lacquered cork poppers are heavier than those made of closed-cell foam or balsa, and those with cup-shaped mouths are easily manipulated to produce plopping sounds that attract attention. In current, they are best cast either up and across or down and across and should be manipulated as fast or as slowly as the stream's flow demands. The bass's responses to them also indicate the need for fast or slow activation. Hold the rod tip just above the surface and remove all slack. In still or slow moving water, holding the rod tip just beneath the surface enhances control of surface flies and facilitates "popping" especially if the weather is breezy, but be certain to set the hook with a firm strip rather than the conventional rod lift. Rapidly lifting the rod from the water can break its tip.

If smallmouths attack the fly vigorously it is an indication that they are located in the upper portion of the water column and are aggressively feeding. Surface flies can be moved quickly so that the angler can cover lots of promising areas in a short time. If the bass seem to rise to the popper in slow motion, then delicately steal the fly; however, they have likely moved from deeper water and might not be actively feeding. As a result, the fly must be maneuvered with more subtlety and long pauses between twitches. Vigorous popper movements are appropriate when frightened minnows are observed spraying into the air in desperate attempts to escape unseen predators. Aggressive swirls indicate active fish in pursuit of prey.

The quality of commercially manufactured poppers differs greatly from one brand to another. We've used some that didn't sit in the water at the proper angle, which affects their ability to pop efficiently. By "efficiently" we mean that poppers shouldn't require long, forceful strips to produce the popping sound. If you purchase commercial poppers, look for those with durable lacquered finishes that will survive frequent contact with rocks.

Many choose to tie their own poppers and one of the best patterns is the AllenLite Popper shown to us by fly-fishing legend Dave Whitlock. Perhaps no one in fly-fishing has created more practical fly-fishing patterns than Dave. We've chosen to include his "eight favorite flies for smallmouth bass."

Dave explains, "My good friend tied the original poppers that inspired this fly. Now that I've used it for several seasons, I've found this fly to be incredibly effective on smallmouth, especially when they are active and respond to flies that create a lot of action and sound. In fact, it has become my 'go-to' surface bass popper fly."

AllenLite Popper (yellow)

Hook: TMC 8089, sizes 10, 6, 2, barb bent down
Thread: yellow Wapsi Ultra Thread 70
Body: Wapsi AllenLite Popper Head, small, medium or large
Skirt: yellow neck hackle (webby and long)
Tail: yellow cock hackle (webby and soft), yellow marabou, gold Flashabou, yellow Krystal Flash
Paint: Body: yellow, fluorescent red, and black acrylic enamel
Eyes: black and white acrylic enamel
Overcoat: clear Wapsi Gloss Coat or clear Hard As Nails
Snag Guard: hard mason nylon (size 10 = 0.018", size 6 = 0.020", size 2 = 0.024")
Cement: Dave's Flexament, Zap-a-Gap and 5-Min-Epoxy

Pencil poppers with elongated bodies can be manipulated to change directions on the retrieve more readily than standard poppers. They maneuver through weeds with fewer hang-ups and their longer bodies more accurately represent the shape and movement of wounded minnows. We most often use white pencil poppers with red details or those with metallic silver finishes.

The use of deer-hair bugs can be traced into smallmouth fly-fishing's history, but they also remain the preferred poppers of many modern fly anglers. They set in, rather than on, the water's surface where stripping them produces unique gurgling sounds that their supporters regard as more natural than that of cork or foam poppers. They are more wind-resistant, and often larger bugs need to be cast by 7- or 8-weight rods. Fly-fishing icon Dave Whitlock and lots of fly anglers are fond of his deer-hair pattern, the Most Whit Hair Bug, for smallmouths. It is effective in a variety of color combinations, but Dave's partial to the one he calls "fruit cocktail" for its visibility to the angler as well as the bass. As he said, "Since its creation I've continually gone to this fly and color when I'm not sure what smallmouth are feeding on when they're at the surface. It's got that classic hair bug shape and the colors that smallmouth can't seem to resist."

Most Whit Hair Bug (fruit cocktail)

Hook: TMC 8089, sizes 20, 6, 2, barb bent down
Thread: yellow Danville Flymaster Plus
Tail: fluorescent yellow marabou; yellow Krystal Flash; green, fluorescent yellow and fluorescent orange rubber hackle; fluorescent yellow and fluorescent green cock neck hackles
Skirt: fluorescent yellow soft cock hackle, yellow Krystal Flash
Legs: black, fluorescent geen, fluorescent yellow, and fluorescent orange rubber hackle
Body: green, black, red, fluorescent yellow and fluorescent orange deer hair
Eyes: yellow and black hollow plastic
Snag Guard and Hook Foundation: hard mason monofilament (size 10 = 0.020", size 6 = 0.022", size 2 = 0.025")
Cement: Dave's Flexament, Goop and Zap-a-Gap
Note: Dave ties this fly in other pattern colors: black and blue, black

and red, black and yellow, black peacock, canary, frog, Porkey's Pet, Would Bee.

The floatability of deer-hair bugs can be improved to last through an entire outing by rubbing dry fly floatant into the fly, drying it with a hand-held blow dryer, then repeating the process. We've used this method for several seasons, but it works so well that we only treat our deer-hair floater/divers once so they'll dive as deeply as we want on the retrieve.

The popper's antithesis, the slider, has a reversed head. Instead of a cupped-face or flat surface head that resists being pulled along the water's surface, it is designed to pass more silently. In thin or very clear water where flies are highly visible to the bass, skittish fish may prefer this subtler fly. One pattern that combines the noiseless retrieve with lifelike rubber legs is "Dave's Sponge Spider," by Dave Whitlock. When asked about his sponge spider, Dave responded, "This is a great fly to use when smallmouth are feeding on terrestrials as well as emerging dragonfly nymphs. For me this fly consistently gets good results with smallmouth in both streams and in lakes, and it's excellent tied in black or brown, too." Here's the recipe:

Dave's Sponge Spider (yellow)

Hook: TMC 2306, size 6, barb bent down
Thread: yellow Wapsi Ultra Thread 140
Snag Guard: Mason hard monofilament (0.020")
Body Foundation: Mason hard monofilament (0.025")
Body Foundation Wrap: pearl Mylar
Body: yellow Wapsi Sponge Spider Foam, large
Legs: medium yellow Wapsi Round Rubber, large
Eyes: 3mm Wapsi yellow doll eyes with black pupils
Cements: Dave's Flexament, Zap-a-Gap, and Goop

We like white, yellow or chartreuse poppers and sliders because they are more visible to us even in fading light and in shadows where they're often fished, but frog-colored patterns can be best during late spring through mid-summer when young-of-the-year naturals are abundant. Despite our preference for the visibility of lighter colors, solid black poppers or sliders can be very effective because they present sharp silhouettes at sunup, after sundown, and on dark, gloomy days.

It bears repeating that observant smallmouth fishermen will catch many more fish. Never is this truer than when fishing the surface. Look for signs of anything available that might interest the bass and be aware of their responses. Is there a hatch coming off the water? Are there smallmouths rising to it? Are there dragonflies hovering over the water, tiny frogs fleeing from your footsteps or minnows spraying into the air? If there are, choose flies that approximate the size and action of their natural counterparts. Let the intensity of surface activity reveal the type of retrieve that should be used. Wild, thrashing activity calls for an aggressive approach while subtle takes indicate that slower, quieter presentations might be necessary.

If we are able to visually locate a fish and observe its activity or even if there is a piece of structure that we suspect harbors a smallmouth, there are two possible approaches to presentation. The most frequently utilized approach calls for casting beyond the targeted area and, either through current drift or manipulation, bringing the fly past the fish into its field of vision. It's quieter, causes fewer disturbances, and enables the angler to implement fly movements at the critical moments when the fly passes the fish's position, but there is yet another viable option. This approach calls for casting the fly right on top of the fish. The sudden intrusion can cause the fish to flee, but smallmouth bass are also very reactionary. They might instinctively turn to and grab something that hits the water near their positions. Whether this behavior is prompted by their opportunistic-feeding or self-preservation instincts is difficult to say, but smallmouths do frequently react in this manner. Smallmouth guide, Duane Hada, agrees, "Yes, I see that all the time. I believe that reactionary movement to a splashdown is even more prevalent with smallmouths than with largemouths." Employing the tactic is exciting because the strike is immediate and aggressive. Finish the cast's follow through with the rod tip low to the water so that the fly will actually "splat" audibly directly above the fish. This "on the nose" presentation isn't the first recommended tactic, but after your best flies and retrieves have been refused rest the fish by not casting to it for a few minutes, then drop a fly right overhead. The results can be surprising.

There are many times when there's not much activity to be observed: no hatches, no hyper minnow activity—the water seems almost asleep. When this happens it's necessary to go prospecting. Often it's an indication that it's time to forsake the surface to probe deeper water, but don't abandon the thrill of topwater action prematurely. Fish may be actively feeding in shallow water but can't be seen because they are located in riffles. The moving water shields them from our view but also enables us to be unseen by them. Smallmouths often use the current breaks in riffles for protection from the force of the water but dart out from behind their rocks to grab prey.

A "skittering" technique can be employed in riffles using pencil poppers to imitate frightened minnows fleeing across the surface. Cast down and across the riffle keeping the rod's tip high and immediately impart stripping and rod maneuvering action to skip the popper across the fast water. Smallmouths that have taken positions behind current breaks in riffles have only an instant to respond so the strikes are explosive. Light-colored pencil poppers with a bit of flash are best for this tactic.

Moths frequently become entrapped in the surface film and wriggle dramatically to try to free themselves and get airborne. Patterns with clipped deer-hair bodies of various colors and white bucktail wings that extend away from the hook shank at a 90-degree angle are easiest to tie. By shaking the rod tip, the wings tend to prevent the fly from moving forward so that it appears to quiver like the natural.

Mice are also the victims of accidental dunkings. They paddle furiously as they make slow progress toward shore. A slow, steady retrieve will create a small wake to replicate the natural.

A "skittering" technique can be employed in riffles to imitate frightened minnows.

Dragonflies and Damselflies

Dragonflies and damselflies, similar in appearance, are among the showiest of aquatic insects. Both sun-loving insects are typically found around lakes, ponds, rivers, and streams. There are more than four hundred species in North America that vary in size up to a wing span of nearly 6 inches. Dragonflies are generally larger than damselflies but they are best identified by the way they position their wings at rest. Dragonflies hold their wings horizontally; damselflies hold them vertically. Many species of dragonflies are beautifully marked with black, dark brown, or gray patterns against red, yellow, blue, or green. Their large eyes are sometimes colored a glowing green or red. Dragonfly wings are heavily veined and sometimes marked with patches of black, brown, white, purple, yellow or red. Capturing them to study their markings isn't an easy task because they are strong fliers. Most of them elude the smallmouths as well. Damselflies are less proficient fliers. Their bodies are more slender and only a few species have colored patches on their wings. Most often, both damselflies and dragonflies are found in bushes, brush, and tree limbs near the water or clinging to the leafy ends of emergent vegetation and the branch tips of deadfalls.

Damselfly duns can be imitated by Elk Hair Caddis patterns in large sizes, such as 6 and 8, with body colors that match the natural, but our favorite pattern for this fishing is an Improved Sofa Pillow. Originally, it was tied to imitate Western stoneflies, but its long, slender body and floatability allow it be fished in a dead drift or skittered across the surface. Many different color combinations can be used but blue, green, and burnt orange are consistent producers. This is our version.

Modified Sofa Pillow

Hook: TMC 5262, sizes 4 through 8
Thread: Black 3/0
Tail and Wing: Light bull elk body hair
Body: Green Uni-stretch thread 1X
Body Hackle: Brown, palmered
Front hackle: Brown
Note: This is a durable pattern that can be dressed with floatant then skated across the water to imitate the action of the naturals. We like to fish it up and across near the heads or tails of pools

just before dark and alongside weedbeds anytime. To impart the proper action, make a short cast to maintain line control and try to keep the rod tip elevated. At regular intervals, strip line to remove slack as the current moves the fly downstream, then make short strips while twitching the rod tip so that the imitation duplicates the erratic struggles of the naturals.

The movement of the fly often triggers the strike, and watching smallmouths chase the manmade imitation can be its own reward. Twenty years ago we spent several weeks each summer camped on the banks of southern Missouri's Bryant Creek. We float-fished from canoes frequently, but many mornings and most evenings found us wet-wading long stretches of the river. One of our favorite pools had a spring that cascaded down a rock wall into the river. To get to it we waded through a hundred yards of pocket water, a graveled shoal, and a partially submerged silt and gravel bar that was covered with leafy, green emergent weeds. Usually, we waded the shallows on the opposite shore and tried to swim streamers past the outside edge of the weedbed. It was seldom the equal of the pocket water upstream, so we hurried through, determined to wade on to the spring pool. One morning as we sloshed along, we noticed dozens of damselflies hovering above the weeds. Smallmouths were rising to those that came close to their positions, while others chased across the pool in a feeding frenzy. We threw everything our vests held that even remotely resembled a damselfly dun to no avail. After a midday session at the tying vice we returned with some crude dry flies with brightly colored elongated bodies that were taken with abandon. The flies that weren't pounded as soon as they hit the water we allowed to dead-drift a couple of feet before slightly twitching our rod tips back and forth so that the fly quivered without much forward movement. The action simulated a damselfly caught in the surface film and it produced some smashing strikes.

The physical similarity between adult damselflies and dragonflies is apparently close enough to fool the bass so we haven't seen the need to imitate both forms. One pattern seems to cover all the bases.

Members of the wasp family that construct mud cell nests are referred to as mud daubers. In summer, when they frequently land on the water's surface to take in water for building their nests, they are vulnerable to bass and panfish. A wide variety of imitations are readily available, but one of the most interesting comes from tyer Mike Huffman. He ties his Mud Dauber this way:

Huffman's Mud Dauber

Hook: Heavy wire scud style, size 6
Abdomen: Black 1/8-inch closed cell sheet foam, 15- to 20-pound mono
Legs: 3 turns of webby black hackle
Wings: 2 brown shiny rooster spade hackle tips tied in delta style. The wings should not extend past the tip of the abdomen.
Thorax: ½-inch by ¾-inch strip of 1/8-inch black closed cell sheet foam
Cement: Super Glue
Tying Instructions: Preassemble abdomen. Burn a nub on the end of the mono. Sandwich the nub between two half squares of sheet foam with superglue. Trim foam into a teardrop shape. Trim the other end of mono to measure one inch, and burn another nub. Tie in abdomen assembly. To tie abdomen: Trim foam to taper down to ¼ inch wide at one end. Tie in the trimmed end. Fold the foam forward, pinch in an inverted "U," push it up ¼ inch, and then secure it with thread wraps to create a humped thorax. Trim foam in front of the wraps and tie off.

The significance of aquatic insect life on the feeding habits of smallmouth bass varies widely. Hatches are generally heavier in the northern half of the smallmouth's range than in the southern portion of it, but even heavy hatches are ignored at times. We've spoken to many guides who discount hatches altogether and prefer instead to imitate more substantial food forms. Still, it's hard to overlook the memorable times when conditions were right and dry flies became the magic potion.

Other Terrestrials

As opportunistic feeders, smallmouth bass seldom fail to capitalize on terrestrial insects that get an unexpected dousing. Ants, beetles, and crickets are potential meals, too, but grasshoppers have the size and bulk to attract heavyweight bronzebacks. Grasshoppers live in pastures and along the grassy edges of fields that border rivers. A breeze over the water can increase the likelihood that they'll end up in the stream. They often land with an inglorious "splat" close to the bank where they try to kick their way to something solid above the waterline before they're swept away by the current. Some collide with midstream rocks and debris before they eventually attempt the big hop to dry land. Fly anglers should be on the lookout for grasshopper hatches from mid-summer into early autumn.

In the mid-1970s we fished a river close to a major metropolitan area that had a reputation for big smallmouth bass but also drew considerable fishing pressure. After taking several 12-inchers by stripping streamer patterns through pocket water, the action turned off. As the sun had risen, a stiff breeze brought relief from the heat. Eventually we waded toward shore and noticed consistent rises at the base of a steep clay embankment. Grasshoppers were being blown over the edge and dropped indelicately on the surface. Almost all were gobbled up in short order. Because of the heat, we had stuffed our pockets with forceps, clippers, extra leaders, and tippet, but only one fly box apiece. Neither contained a hopper pattern, but we did find a couple of Muddler Minnows. We cast them into the feeding lane with enough force to make audible splats. We caught several smallmouths, including a fat 16-incher, before the gusty breeze abated and the oppressive heat forced us off the stream.

Most species of grasshoppers are winged and many are skilled fliers, including some that are migratory, but stiff breezes force them off course and some end up in the water. One pattern will likely suffice for matching hoppers but it's best to carry several sizes and colors that suggest the naturals in the area.

A bit of a breeze across high, grassy banks above rocky structure can stimulate the bass even on large impoundments. Our choice of patterns to imitate grasshoppers is the Western Hopper designed by Harrison Steeves and modified by Missouri guide Jim Murphy. It floats and fishes like Mother Nature's version.

Murphy's Western Hopper

Hook: TMC 7989, size 6
Thread: Tan UTC 140
Tail: Tan UV Krystal Flash
Underbody: Tan 1/16-inch Evazote strip cut the width of the hook gap
Overbody: Gray 1/16-inch Evazote strip cut to the width of the hook gap
Ribbing: Brown size A thread for rod winding
Legs: Brown medium round rubber legs
Underwing: Tan UV Krystal Flash
Wing: Natural deer body hair
Overwing: Natural turkey tail, one segment split after fly is finished
Thorax: Tan super fine dubbing
Head: Tan 3/16-inch diameter disc 2mm cross-link foam
Eyes: Chartreuse EZ Shape Sparkle Body

We also like St-Louis-area tyer Joe Amoinette's large sponge spider with rubber legs as a searching pattern. When fished in relatively flat water, it floats high and it has an attractive wiggly action.

Joe's Sponge Spider

Hook: Mustad 3366 or equivalent, size 6
Thread: 3/0 chartreuse Monocord
Tail: Red feather tips or short red yarn
Body: Black 3-inch piece of 3/8-inch closed cell foam
Wing: Chartreuse deer hair
Legs: Two 4-inch chartreuse rubber legs

Floater/Divers

In the early 1960s the spin-casters' hottest bass lure was a floating Rapala. At that time, it represented a new concept in fishing: a plug that wiggled on the retrieve and floated at rest. The limitations on innovative presentations were confined only by the imagination of the angler. As fish after fish fell for the new lure, it became clear that fly-fishers would profit from duplication of the Rapala. Tiny models were created for the purpose, but they were difficult to cast accurately, especially in the wind, and most fly-fishers rejected them.

Then Minnesotan Don Gapen wrote about the success he'd had dressing Muddler Minnows with floatant so they could be fished in a similar fashion to Rapala-casting spin fishermen. Finally the gap had been bridged, but it took a decade more for Larry Dahlberg to clip a spun deer-hair head for the purpose of making the fly dive on the retrieve. Eventually, after much body redesign the Dahlberg Diver became the fly-fisher's answer to floater/divers. Because the tail materials are flexible, the Dahlberg Diver looks even more enticing in the water than the original balsa minnow. They are effective when tied to represent wounded minnows by using white tail feathers and white deer hair with a bit of added silver Krystal Flash or tied in blue, olive, yellow, and orange deer hair to represent small sunfishes.

Two of our favorite patterns are tied to represent a swimming frog. When tiny frogs begin hopping across the gravel bars in late spring and throughout the summer they are the best big smallmouth surface fly in our boxes. Bass Pro Shop's Mike Huffman ties this natural-colored version.

Whitlock's Diving Frog (modified)

Hook: Straight eye wide gap, TMC 8089 or equivalent, size 6
Kickers: Six splayed rooster hackles, wide and webby, color to match the body
Collar: Six turns of hackle to match the kickers
Legs: Three strands rubber legs
Body: Deer hair trimmed flat on the bottom. Front 2/3 is trimmed like a half-bullet. Rear 1/3 is trimmed as a collar.
Eyes: Solid plastic craft eyes with stems trimmed off and glued into place.
Note: Results are better if sockets are trimmed or burned for eyes to rest in.

Small frogs sit motionless in slack water awaiting hapless insects to come within tongue-flicking range. They duck underwater and kick vigorously when they sense danger, then float back to the surface usually after swimming only a foot or two. It's after this brief swim that they are most vulnerable to bass. We imitate this action by "double pumping" our flies. We make a foot-long strip to pull the frog under, then move the rod tip in the same direction as the fly's path a few inches so that the fly seems to kick a second time. Sometimes the strike occurs when the fly resurfaces, but frequently a telltale bronze flash indicates the phony frog has been intercepted as it swims. If not, we let it rest for approximately 10 seconds then repeat the process. Dave Whitlock shared another more brightly colored version with us, adding "I originally designed this fly color pattern to entice smallmouth living in darkly-stained waters, but soon discovered that it was equally effective in clear water. It's also just a lot of fun to fish with. My largest smallmouth on a surface diver came to this fly pattern and was an incredible 23-3/4 inches !". Here's "Dave's Orange-belly Diving Frog:"

Dave's Orange-belly Diving Frog

Hook: TMC 8089, sizes 10, 6, 2, barb bent down
Thread: fluorescent orange Danville Single Strand Flat Floss
Legs: fluorescent orange neck hackle, grizzly dyed fluorescent green neck hackle
Skirt: orange Krystal Flash, fluorescent orange neck hackle
Front Legs: fluorescent orange rubber hackle, fluorescent green rubber hackle, black rubber hackle
Collar: fluorescent orange deer body hair, fluorescent green deer body hair, black deer body hair
Head: fluorescent orange deer body hair, fluorescent green deer body hair, black deer body hair
Eyes: green and black solid plastic eyes
Snag-guard and Hook Foundation: Mason hard nylon (size 10 = 0.019", size 6 = 0.022", size 2 = 0.025")
Cement: Dave's Flexament, Goop, Zap-a-Gap
Note: Dave's other pattern colors for his diving frog are white belly and yellow belly.

Our "Wilson's Hula Diver" uses a Dahlberg-style head combined with a tantalizing Sili-leg tail for lots of movement. It's fooled plenty of sassy smallmouths for us.

Wilson's Hula Diver
(fluorescent yellow with orange head)

Hook: Tiemco 8089 or equivalent, size 6 or 10
Thread: orange UNI Big Thread
Tail: 12 strands chartreuse/fire orange Sili Legs each twice the length of the hook shank
Butt: medium orange chenille

Body: fluorescent yellow deer belly hair and orange deer belly hair

The fly is also effective in white with a red head, fluorescent chartreuse with a red head, and purple with a pink head.

Fascination with the explosive surface strikes of smallmouth bass is a strong incentive to fish topwater.

The surface flies we use most often are poppers and floater/ divers. Damselflies, dragonflies, caddisflies, mayflies, and stoneflies are used occasionally depending on the smallmouths' response to whatever insect activity we observe. It's a good idea to carry a few impressionistic patterns so as not to miss out on hatch bonanzas that present themselves every now and then. To us, there's nothing more frustrating than seeing smallmouths rising everywhere, recognizing the prey they're feeding upon, and being unable to interest a single fish.

Fascination with the explosive surface strike provides a strong incentive to fish topwater flies, and we are as guilty as any anglers of staying with surface presentations too long. While all fly-fishers need to be reminded that smallmouths feed beneath the water's surface far more regularly, it's wise to stay alert to any of the subtle signs that indicate aggressive smallmouths might be taken on top.

CHAPTER 7
MID-DEPTH TACTICS AND FLIES

While the term shallow implies a reasonable proximity to the surface and deep is commonly associated with the bottom, defining the mid-depths is more abstract. Mid-depth could be as shallow as a foot of water or less, but it could also be a hundred feet or more. While those wide parameters might qualify as a definition, practically speaking, 20 feet is a much more common maximum depth. The implication is that flies must be stripped, trolled or drifted through the mid-depths without either returning to the surface or bumping along the bottom. Our mid-depth flies tend to imitate minnows, leeches, and nymphs that drift toward the surface to hatch, such as mayflies and caddisflies. We also use three specialty flies that perform well for us in the mid-depths that do not represent specific smallmouth bass fare. Each of these flies is capable of producing movement that's independent of manipulation as it's swept along by the current or as it falls through still water before it's activated by the angler.

Smallmouths that capitalize on mid-depth feeding opportunities are active feeders and are therefore very catchable. Nymph-feeding river smallmouths might be located behind a current break waiting to rush out and grab any morsel that comes in sight while stillwater bronzebacks might be suspended or cruising over the lake bottom in search of a meal.

Fishing the mid-depths can be the drag-free drift of a size-16 mayfly nymph at a foot deep below a riffle, but it might also mean dropping a sparsely tied Clouser Minnow into 15 feet of stillwater over a 35-foot bottom. For many anglers, fishing the mid-depths of stillwater is a disorienting experience because most of our fishing has conditioned us to be very dependent upon seeing structure at the water's surface. Casting to open water in which we can't see our flies or feel the bottom can be perplexing at first.

Floating line isn't very practical beyond a depth of approximately 4 feet in stillwater and, depending on current speed, that depth might be less in moving water. Getting flies deeper can be accomplished by extending the length of the leader, but this option quickly reaches a point of diminishing returns when casting is affected. Heavy flies on light, flexible tippets are difficult to control, especially when the weather is breezy. Sink-tip and full-sinking lines are more efficient for handling the mid-depths deeper than 4 feet. With a few exceptions, our tackle includes floating lines with 6- to 9- foot leaders and sink-tip or full-sinking lines with 3-1/2 to 9-foot leaders. Shorter leaders are used with flies that aren't heavy enough to prevent them from buoying back toward the surface, which defeats the purpose of sinking lines. We use long leaders on sinking lines in very clear water with relatively heavy flies.

The most important consideration in selecting tippet size is water clarity. In spring creeks and clear lakes we use 5X tippet most frequently, but if leader shyness appears to be the problem it might be necessary to switch to 6X. Long leaders with light tippets and heavy flies are necessary in some exceptionally clear water where fish might be leader-shy. Tippet hinging on the cast can be a problem, of course, and heavy flies on light tippets are recommended only as the last resort. While fishing a spring creek in north central Arkansas, we cast heavily weighted Clouser variations on 5X tippets. We quickly learned that heavier tippets or lighter flies failed to produce hits and we were forced to cast the unwieldy combination. Fast-tipped rods turned those lead-laced flies into dangerous, misguided missiles while rods with soft tips enabled us to complete short, lobbing casts with relatively soft splashdowns.

Nymphs fished in the mid-depths can be very productive in moving water.

Mid-Depth Nymphing

Smallmouths feed on nymphs at mid-depth in moving water because they provide easy, reliable meals. We seldom use mid-depth nymphs in still water because they attract too many sunfish and thus slow the search for smallmouths. Mid-depth stream nymphs include mayflies and caddisflies. To replicate them we favor impressionistic patterns, but we readily admit that many other patterns can be successful. We named our mayfly imitation the North Fork Nymph because it evolved from several "rock turning" episodes in a southern Missouri river by the same name. Most of the mayfly nymphs we found in the stream looked enough like the fly to fool many fish over the years. It's simply our own adaptation of mid-twentieth century English river keeper Frank Sawyer's Pheasant Tail Nymph. We tie it "in the round" (without a carapace) so that as it tumbles through the current it will appear natural.

North Fork Nymph

Hook: TMC 200R, sizes 10-16
Tail: Pheasant tail fibers
Abdomen: Same pheasant tail fibers wrapped around thread that is then wrapped around the hook shank
Thorax Underbody: 5 to 6 turns of .020 lead wire (optional)
Thorax: Natural fox squirrel dubbing
Legs: pick out guard hairs from thorax
Head: brown 6/0 thread

We fish the North Fork Nymph at the lower parts of riffles, in pocket water with moderate current, and in the tailouts of pools. Cast upstream and allow the fly to sink to the desired depth or cast it up and across at an angle determined by the speed of the current so that drag doesn't overtake the fly too quickly. In slow currents, down-and-across casts can be effective. At the end of a down-and-across dead drift when the fly is affected by drag and begins to rise to the surface, it might appear to the fish that the nymph is about to emerge as a dun. Many strikes occur in this portion of the drift if current speed is slow enough to permit the nymph imitation to get deep into the water column. A reach cast and mending lengthen the drag-free drift and enable the fly to reach deeper into the water column.

We use two caddisfly nymph patterns. The first is a simple soft hackle fly. Soft hackle flies date back to the second century A.D. and consist only of a floss or dubbed body and a sparsely wound breast or flank feather from a partridge, quail, grouse, woodcock or starling. Sylvester Nemes revitalized these popular flies in his book *The Soft-Hackled Fly*.

When a bit of flash is needed to attract the bass's attention or when we use it as an attractor pattern, we like a bead fly pattern tied by smallmouth enthusiast and rod builder John Henry that's proven irresistible on stream smallmouths. Here's the way John ties his Bead Body Bass Buster:

Bead Body Bass Buster

Hook: TMC 100, sizes 10 through 12
Thread: 8/0 brown
Body: 5 seed beads, mustard yellow color
Hackle: Brown 8/0

These patterns should be fished in rock and gravel sections of a stream that have at least moderate current where natural nymphs live. Sometimes caddis patterns are taken by hungry smallmouths when abundant hatches are present. The aquatic forms of caddisflies are actually larval and pupal, but fly-fishers refer to them as nymphs nonetheless.

The upstream, up-and-across, and down-and across-presentations previously described in Chapter 3 work with caddisfly patterns as well. Many anglers prefer to use a strike indicator or a fluorescent mono section to connect the fly line to the leader to help them detect hits. The most difficult aspect of any dead drifted fly presentation is strike detection. Short casts of 25 feet or less are necessary to maintain control of the fly. Long casts make strike detection and good hook-sets more difficult. Smallmouths suck in nymphs but they are capable of rejecting phony ones with hooks in them very quickly. Slack line or late strike detection dramatically reduces the number of hook-ups.

Getting within 25 feet of the bass in clear water increases the risk of spooking them. Swift water helps to some degree in concealing the angler, but care must be taken in choosing casting locations and getting into position for nymphing. A little planning should be done in advance of the first cast. Try to determine where the bass will be and which position must be taken to make the best presentation.

Mid-Depth Minnows

Minnows provide smallmouth bass with meals that are higher in calories than any of their other menu items. Since bass and minnows seek food and cover in the same places, minnows are convenience food. Smallmouths often cruise near weedbeds and wood structure that attract foraging minnows or they take up positions where intercepting minnows are likely possibilities.

There are many different species of minnows that occupy smallmouth water. Anglers tend to classify the fry of game fish as minnows, which further expands the list. Matching the minnows in the waters you fish regularly is one productive concept, but we prefer a more impressionistic approach for its versatility.

Chubs frequently occupy the faster sections of streams. The term chub is a colloquialism in the eastern United States for the fallfish and it is commonly used to refer to a large number of fishes of the family Cyprinidae. Anglers often see the silvery flashes of chubs' sides as they feed in swift currents and may have hooked some when fishing small nymphs in riffles and pool tailouts. As their name implies, they have chunky bodies and they are readily available to smallmouth bass that feed in fast water.

Our favorite pattern for matching chubs is a bead head Krystal Bugger in white with a bit of silver Krystal Flash in the tail. We first used it in the Kiamichi Mountains with guide Rob Woodruff. The size of the bead head can be adjusted so that the fly's weight is right for the current speed and depth. Here's the recipe for Rob's Krystal Bugger:

Rob's Krystal Bugger (white)

Hook: Mustad 3366, size 4 or Mustad 9672
Thread: White 3/0 Uni-thread
Tail: Silver Krystal Flash surrounded by white marabou, both the length of the hook shank (Arctic fox can be substituted for the marabou)
Body: pearl Long Ice Chenille
Head: 3/16-diameter nickel bead
Note: Rob sometimes uses Arctic fox for the tail in place of marabou. He also substitutes a Mustad 9672 hook to give the fly a longer body.

If the riffle we've chosen to fish is shallow, we cast down and across to allow the fly to swing across the current on a tight line before imparting short, darting strips. Allow the current to drift the fly back into the starting position before repeating the strips. Deep, fast riffles can be approached in two ways. Cast slack line well above the targeted area and then allow the line to tighten as the fly sinks so that it can be manipulated at the desired depth. To try the other option, cast upstream into the riffle and fish the fly by lifting, then lowering, the rod tip to control the inevitable slack line. Casts from either position must be short enough that line and fly control will permit a good hook-set. Other than by depth and current speed, casting positions are dictated by the location that's least likely to spook the fish.

Our earliest smallmouth bass success came while stripping a Black Nosed Dace through rocky pools. The pattern still takes lots of fish for us, but now we prefer the all marabou version tied by South Carolinian Doug Farthing.

Marabou Black Nosed Dace

Hook: streamer hook 6XL sizes 4 through 6
Thread: Black
Body: Flat silver tinsel
Rib: Silver oval tinsel
Tail: Red marabou
Underwing: Approximately 8 white deer tail hairs
Wing: Equal parts of white and tan marabou on top, black marabou in the middle

For a mid-pool searching pattern we prefer a pretty hackled streamer tied by Louisiana tyer Marc Pinsel. Marc's Magic Minnow is an impressionistic pattern with a strong silhouette and good action.

Marc's Magic Minnow

Hook: Partridge CS52, size 8 stainless steel salt hook
Thread: Black 6/0
Wings: 2 Whiting Lace hackle feathers two times the length of the hook shank
Tail: Whiting White Lace feathers
Body: Tightly wrapped White Lace feather palmered densely
Underwing: 5 strands flat silver tinsel
Overwing: 15 strands of peacock herl almost as long as the tail
Throat: red Krystal Flash

Marc's Magic Minnow can be fished shallow on floating line or deep on sink-tip or full-sinking line in moving or still water. Retrieves using erratic strips of varying lengths followed by pauses that allow the fly to settle back into the fish zone are effective, as are change-of-direction retrieves which not only simulate fleeing baitfishes, but in stillwater also present the fly's silhouette to fish from different angles.

In stillwater, schools of smallmouths migrate with shad and ambush them periodically when the baitfishes can be herded into places where they're vulnerable near land or at the water's surface. Observant anglers watch for the shad schools spraying into the air in wild attempts to escape. Often such surface attacks are initiated by other species of bass but smallmouths pursue these migrant meals just as enthusiastically. The slashing assaults create injured minnows that flutter toward the bottom where the biggest bass often await their easy banquet just below the crowd. To capitalize on this fishing opportunity, we use a fly created especially for these shad-burst bass. The fly is called the Squirrel-Spin 2K for our modification of our usual pattern.

Squirrel-Spin 2K

Hook: Tiemco 8089 or equivalent, size 8 or 12"
Thread: gray 6/0
Trailer: size 00 silver Colorado spinner blade with barrel swivel and ring
Underbody: gray wool yarrn
Body: silver Quick Descent dubbing
Rib: silver medium Ultra Wire
Gills: red medium chenille
Wings: clump of gray squirrel tail
Head: small nickel cone head, Quick Descent dubbing to fill gap

One of the most effective of all minnow imitators is the Clouser Minnow originated by Bob Clouser. Barbell eyes cause the fly to ride hook point up which helps keep it from hanging up too frequently. Clouser Minnows can be tied in a variety of weights to suit the depth of the water. We use the extra small size (1/50 ounce) and fish it on full-sinking line when it's necessary to get the fly deep quickly in reservoirs. In clear water it's important to tie Clousers sparsely, while stained water requires a larger clump of throat and wing material. A more substantial silhouette is easier for the bass to see and its bulkiness displaces more water so it's easier for them to locate by sound. Retired Bass Pro Shop's Fly-fishing Specialist Terry Tanner ties our favorite pattern, which is modified from the original.

Tanner's Kraft-Hair Minnow (Duskystripe Shiner)

Hook: Mustad 455 spinner bait hook, size 8 nickel
Thread: Gray or pale green 8/0
Eyes: Small painted brass dumbbell eyes
Belly: Silver or white Kraft-Fur
Sides or Middle Body: Gray Kraft-Fur with pearl or olive Midge Krystal Flash
Top Wing or Back: Medium olive Kraft-Fur

Tanner developed these smaller Clousers using Kraft-Fur rather than the original's bucktail because Kraft-Fur undulates in the water better when it's cut in smaller lengths. Whatever color variations are used should graduate from light at the belly to a darker color on the back. Remember, this fly is designed so that it rides hook point up in the water. Tanner attaches the eyes farther back along the hook shank to give the fly more realistic action.

Clousers are effective in a variety of colors, but selecting fly color depends on water clarity. The natural, gray/white, is best in clear water while chartreuse/white is more visible to the fish in stained water. The inevitable repeated contact with rocks results in broken deer hair and chipped, dented eyes, which causes conventional Clousers to look beaten up. We add EZ Shape Sparkle Body around the heads of some of our patterns to increase their

Clousers are effective flies that can be easily tied in a variety of colors.

durability in fast, rock-strewn waters. Clousers are equally effective in deeper pools of moving water and in stillwater when they're counted down. Sparsely tied Clousers fished in very clear lakes to suspended, minnow-feeding smallmouths can be exceptional producers. Electronic locators are indispensable in determining the depth at which the flies need to be fished.

We've had great success with a couple of our baitfish imitations we call "Wilson's Lil' Shad" and "Wilson's Lil' Sunfish."

Wilson's Lil' Shad

Hook: Tiemco 8089 or equivalent, size 10 or 12
Thread: gray 3/0
Tail: Ultrasuede, ½-inch cut to shape, colored with metallic silver pen
Underbody: gray wool yarn to enlarge body
Over body: silver Quick Descent dubbing
Rib: silver medium Ultra Wire
Eyes: gold with black pupil extra small barbell eyes
Wings (top and bottom): clumps of white Polar Fibre extending just past the hook's bend
Head: gray sculpin wool

When the fly is tied with a copper body, olive wings, and red barbell eyes it becomes "Wilson's Lil' Sunfish."

Another minnow in our fly boxes is a pattern originated by the late Gary LaFontaine as shown to North Carolina guide David Duffy. It's called the Drop Nose Minnow. Here's his modified version:

Drop Nose Minnow

Hook: Mustad 3366 sizes 6 through 1/0
Bead head: 3/16 brass bead
Thread: Olive Uni-thread 8/0
Tail: 6 to 8 strands of chartreuse Krystal Flash as long as the distance from the hook eye to the hook point, burnt orange marabou as long as the hook from the bend to the eye.
Rear body: (which covers 2/3 of the hook shank) 3 to 4 strands of chartreuse Krystal Flash twisted into a dubbing loop with medium olive Gary LaFontaine's Touch Dubbing wound forward around the hook shank
Underwing: Tan calf tail extending to the hook bend
Wing: Burnt orange marabou the length of the tail topped with 4 strands of peacock herl and 4 strands of chartreuse Krystal Flash
Front body: 4 to 6 strands long peacock herl
Hackle: Brown, palmered

The Drop Nose Minnow is especially effective in slow or still-water. Cast it on a slack line and allow it to reach or at least approach the bottom. Lift the rod tip to cause the fly to rise, then lower the rod and remove the slack line. Repeat this lifting and dropping action until the fly needs to be recast.

In his home waters in the foothills of the Smoky Mountains, Duffy also ties and fishes a "cross breed" fly originated by Susquehanna River guide, instructor, and author Harry Murray, who wrote *Fly Fishing for Smallmouth Bass*. Murray combined parts of some of the best nymph and streamer patterns then let the smallmouths choose which were most attractive. The result was Murray's Strymph. It suggests a wide variety of nymphs and streamers depending on its color and the way it's manipulated. Duffy prefers the fly tied in black, olive, and cream.

Murray's Strymph

Hook: Mustad 9672 or TMC 5262, sizes 2 to 8
Thread: 3/0 pre-waxed monocord, color to match the body
Body: Black, cream, or olive rabbit fur
Tail: Ostrich herl to match the body
Collar: Speckled Indian hen saddle hackle
Weight: Lead wire

Dead-drifted Strymphs are taken as nymphs, but when they are stripped the smallmouth bass mistake them for minnows. We've used them with great success as droppers on tandem rigs below poppers.

One of the most versatile streamers is the Muddler Minnow. It can be used to represent bass prey that ranges from grasshoppers on the surface, when it's dressed with floatant, to bottom-hugging sculpins. Adding marabou to the pattern gives the traditional fly an action that's very attractive to smallmouths.

Leeches

Leeches are present in most lakes and the slow sections of many rivers. Their undulating action is so attractive to smallmouths that they rarely pass up the opportunity to eat them. It's important to swim the fly in a way that imitates the snakelike movements of the naturals. Lifting the rod tip slowly then stripping slowly to remove slack line as the rod tip is lowered imitates the unique swimming motion of leeches. These patterns lose their effectiveness if they are fished too rapidly. A change of direction can also be incorporated into the retrieve to accentuate its allure. Nebraska tyer Elmer Meiler created one of our favorite leech patterns. It's been productive for us in black and olive.

Meiler's Pine Squirrel Leech

Hook: Mustad 9672 or TMC 5263 or Daiichi 1720
Head: Small brass cone head
Tail: Pine Squirrel strip about 1-½ times the length of the hook shank glued in place on the top of the back half with CA+. Tie in Matuka style with medium gold oval tinsel
Rear Body: Medium gold Mylar
Front body: Collar: Coastal deer hair
Body: Coastal deer hair spun or stacked

Other Mid-Depth Flies

There are some flies that aren't designed to represent any food source in particular but are responsible for catching lots of big smallmouths nonetheless. Originally tied as a largemouth bass fly, Rob's W.I.T.H. Bugger, tied on smaller hooks, is equally efficient with smallmouths. East Texas-based guide, entomologist, and fly tyer Rob Woodruff, who guides smallmouth fly-fishers in southeastern Oklahoma, combined the action and materials of several effective bass flies. We've had great success with it in both still and moving water in dissimilar areas of the country. The fly works best when it's allowed to sink into relatively slow pocket water and then is retrieved with alternating strips and pauses. Our best results have come from the smoke-colored version, but brown/gold, and black/orange are effective as well.

Rob's W.I.T.H. Bugger

Hook: TMC 8089, size 10
Head: 3/16-inch Wapsi Cyclops Eye
Thread: Gray Danville flat waxed nylon
Legs: 9 gray Wapsi Sili Legs or other silicone leg material
Body: Gray medium chenille

Hackle: Light dun rooster saddle
Tail: Gray marabou

Another fly that has produced great results especially in spring creeks is Terry Tanner's New Guinea Bugger. Here's Terry's recipe for this colorful fly.

Terry's New Guinea Bugger

Hook: TMC 200R size 6
Thread: 8/0 Uni Thread
Body weight: .020 lead wire
Tail: Marabou
Body: DMC embroidery thread or Uni Stretch
Hackles: 3 spotted Guinea body feathers

Terry's favorite colors include orange/black in stained water, olive/black in clear water, and purple/black in low light conditions. The New Guinea Bugger can be fished in a variety of ways. One of the fly's most productive retrieves is drifting it down and across through pocket water on full-sinking line. After counting down the fly, lift the rod tip a few inches then lower the rod tip but strip only to remove slack before repeating the process.

One of the simplest mid-depth flies is also one of our most consistent producers. The Bead Head Peacock Woolly Bugger is particularly effective for smallmouth bass in cold water and is the fly we use most often in wintertime spring creeks, in the early spring, and late fall. Among warmwater fly-fishers in the Ozarks, Peacock Woolly Buggers are considered a fly-box staple because they are effective for largemouth and smallmouth bass, sunfish, and trout. For best results, fish it on sink-tip or full-sinking line using a dead drift with intermittent twitches of the rod tip. Strip only to recover slack. Erratic, short twitches of the rod tip work well, too.

Bead Head Peacock Woolly Bugger

Hook: TMC 200R, size 10
Tail: Black marabou the length of the hook shank
Body: Peacock herl dyed bright green (We use 4 or 5 pieces wrapped around thread to strengthen.) Regular peacock herl may be used.
Hackle: Neck hackle size 12 brown, palmered
Head: Size 1/8 brass bead

This version of the Woolly Bugger is a dynamite searching pattern. It can be tied without hackle or it can be heavily weighted. It is often tied with a yellow/olive marabou tail. Krystal Flash can be used in the tail, but be aware the material is stiffer and may interfere with the lifelike action of the soft marabou. We also tie a very heavy version with a tail of orange marabou on top and olive marabou on the bottom and fish it using the "crayfish hop" explained in Chapter 8.

Mid-depth Presentation Under Deadfalls In Current

Our preference when fishing the mid-depths is a down-and-across presentation that adjusts the weight of the fly and line to control the depth of the retrieve, but there are situations when current flow and existing structure require a different approach. One such situation, the large, tangled deadfall, gives anglers considerable difficulty. If the current has scoured a hole on the deadfall's downstream side, it's sure to be a big bass hangout. The trouble is that any cast and subsequent drift is guaranteed to leave the branches underneath the structure decorated with flies and tippet material. After a few broken leaders and lost flies, the smallmouth population is likely to ignore further offerings.

While fishing southern Missouri's Big Piney River with the late Hank Reifeiss, who was a highly skilled smallmouth fly-fisher, we were shown a very efficient method of presenting mid-depth flies under large deadfalls. He tied on an unweighted fly and attached a small split shot a few inches above it. This provided just enough weight to get the fly to the desired depth. After assessing the depth of the water under the deadfall, he attached a strike indicator and placed himself just above the pile of wood. He then stripped out enough line to drift the fly beneath and held the rod tip high to keep the current from sweeping his slack line downstream. The fly swiftly drifted under the entanglements as the strike indicator kept the current from forcing the fly into jutting branches and exposed tree roots. Subtle action was imparted at intervals of his choosing. Generally, we prefer not to use strike indicators, but in this situation they can produce some rewarding fish that are otherwise unreachable.

Creative fly tyers have long experimented with making their own fly lips to add action to their flies. Lipped flies add a swimming action to standard fly patterns that duplicate the wobbling motion bait-casters have utilized for decades. Fly lips can be made from several materials, but we prefer those made from thin plastic. Many fly-fishers avoid using them because the lips require occasional "tuning," or bending to adjust their action in the water. Despite this minor inconvenience, they are very productive when used on topwater with floating lines or mid-depth flies that are fished with sink-tip or full-sinking lines. In addition to attaching lips below hooks' shanks, they can be tied in on top for a different action.

Another fly action-enhancing concept is the "Magic Head," a flexible cup that covers the fly head which allows the fly to be fished traditionally, or, when the cup is flipped forward, makes the fly dart from side to side with a lifelike escaping minnow action. Flat round Mylar discs attached behind the hook eyes have been used by warmwater fly fishermen for many years to add action and sound to their flies. Both components add interest to fly tying and fish catching for bass anglers.

Tandem Flies

Another very effective mid-depth presentation involves fishing two flies in tandem. The cast of double flies can involve two nymph patterns, a pair of streamers or a surface fly, such as a popper, and a dropper fly. The nymph and streamer combination might consist of the same patterns to simulate an opportunity for the smallmouth bass to take advantage of abundance or the combination might be two different imitations of forage so that the fish can indicate their preference. While searching for the flies that produce hits, a nymph/streamer tandem might also be utilized. A large streamer that imitates a bass fry or minnow might be used with a nymph to simulate a baitfish chasing its food. The popper/dropper combination enables the popper to double as a strike indicator that suspends the wet pattern at the desired depth. Often, the popper is manipulated to create a disturbance to attract smallmouths that would otherwise not be inclined to come near enough to the surface to hit the dropper fly. When selecting flies for the "popper-with-a-dropper" tandem rig, experiment to learn how large the popper must be to remain on the surface while suspending the dropper fly. If deerhair bugs or floater/diver flies are substituted for the popper, it may be advantageous to the fly's manipulation if the dropper partially submerges the surface bug.

Two options exist for attaching the dropper to the first or main fly. Both involve attaching the tippet to the hook eye of the first fly in the conventional manner. The first method of dropper attachment involves sliding the knot of the first fly to the side of the hook eye, then tying on a second piece of tippet through the same hook eye for the dropper. The second attachment method involves tying the dropper's tippet to the hook bend of the main fly. An improved clinch knot holds the dropper securely, whichever attachment option is chosen.

Another important consideration is the length of the dropper's tippet. The prevailing fishing conditions dictate the parameters, but usually 12 to 24 inches is easiest for the fly-caster to control.

All gamefish are competitive when it comes to feeding. Often when anglers are playing a fish they notice another or several others chasing the hooked fish. Smallmouth bass may even peck at the fly stuck in the corner of the fighting fish's mouth in an attempt to steal the morsel. Tandem rigs offer the unique possibility of catching two fish at once. On North Carolina's Toe River, we hooked and landed a 14-inch and a 10-inch smallmouth on a tandem rig. It was a memorable fight.

Some of the swifter sections of pocket water found in many streams with especially jagged rocks make bottom contact presentations virtually impossible. That, coupled with the smallmouth's capacity for hiding near the bottom, while remaining focused on whatever occurs overhead, makes the mid-depths of rivers especially rewarding. In lakes, the mid-depths are equally important as smallmouths cruise in search of food. Developing confidence in fishing the mid-depths efficiently will add more large smallmouths to your catch-and-release count.

CHAPTER 8
BOTTOM TACTICS AND FLIES

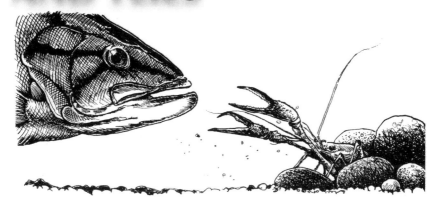

It's hard to understate the importance of rock structure to smallmouth bass. Even in rock-lined lakes, smallmouth bass will utilize rock piles with the most size-diversity, which may range from gravel to enormous boulders. The smallmouth bass's coloration allows it to blend into its environment, and a reliable food source is always available nearby. Smallmouths, whether in moving or still water, relate to this bottom cover a high percentage of the time. As anglers, this is the most important area of the water body to us and we should be proficient in presenting our offerings.

Sometimes bottom structure is located close to the surface, but in clear lakes the structure might be very deep. Clearly, some practical definitions must apply. Deep fishing, with regard to smallmouth bass, implies regular contact with the bottom and therefore regular contact with rocks. The process of fishing deep water carries its own set of problems. First, with flies repeatedly hitting rocks, hook points can become dull very quickly. As with flies for other species of bass, durable hooks are essential. Hook points need to be checked and sharpened repeatedly while fishing or simply tie on fresh flies. Second, tippets are constantly rubbed against the edges of rocks and thus become nicked and rough sometimes after only a few casts. Leaders, too, must be checked and replaced frequently. Finally, the problem of flies getting hung up on rocks needs to be addressed. Sometimes the fly gets wedged in a crevice and just can't be freed, but most often the fly is simply trapped behind a rock by tension from the line and current. A roll cast aimed beyond the hang-up is often all that's necessary to free the fly so it can be recast.

When bottom contact is a consistent element in fly presentation, current speed becomes a critical factor in preventing hang-ups while maintaining contact with the bottom. In swift pocket water for example, bottom contact might only be at 2 feet deep. In clear, still water deep might be less than 5 feet, but conceivably it could be much deeper. Our self-imposed limit for fishing deep water is a maximum of 20 feet. While flies can be presented much deeper, it becomes an act of vertical jigging in which the joy of fly-casting is lost. In addition, even with full-sinking 6-rated line, at least 46 seconds are required to reach the bottom at 20 feet. Impatience weighs heavily enough when fishing at that depth without trying to extend it further. The self-imposed 20-foot limit also makes sense because the thermocline in summer isn't usually much deeper ranging from 20 to 30 feet. Our definition of deep water for smallmouth fishing is making consistent bottom contact between depths of 2 and 20 feet.

There are times when floating line can be used effectively to fish bottom structure. In moving water, depending on current speed, floating line and a leader of 9 feet can accommodate depths of 2 to 5 feet. These parameters cover many moving water situations, but there are some exceptions. In heavy current it may be necessary to change to sink-tip line to keep the fly in the fish zone. It might also be desirable to present the fly with more horizontal movement than floating line would allow. Our use of sink-tip line is limited to shallow swift currents, slightly deeper, slower currents in 4 to 5 feet of water, and some presentations in still water to a depth of 5 to 8 feet.

For any presentation to deeper structure or when horizontal fly movement is necessary, we use full-sinking lines. This means that a high percentage of the time we use floating lines in moving waters, full-sinking lines in stillwater, and sink-tip lines to fish anything in between. While this is our rule of thumb, there are exceptions. If, for example, we want to fish a sculpin pattern along a gravel bar in 2 or 3 feet of water, we would use full-sinking line because of the desired angle of the fly's retrieve. So, while depth helps determine line selection, the decision may be altered by the presentation.

Many fly casters avoid using sinking lines. Some even declare themselves dry fly aficionados so they can sidestep the issue altogether. Most anglers enjoy the thrill of a surface strike, but most fish feed there only about 10 percent of the time. Smallmouth anglers who marry the surface will have a few spectacular days and many in which hook-ups are few and far between. The problem with sinking lines is that their weight keeps them submerged making them difficult to pick up and recast without stripping back most of the line.

The Half-Roll, Open Loop Cast

For years we've used what we've come to call the half-roll, open loop cast. It's very simple to perform, and with just a bit of practice it eliminates the frustration of picking up sinking line. To execute the half-roll, open loop cast, begin by making a long strip with the line hand while lifting the rod tip to the 12 o'clock position. The strip and lift will help to break the tension of the water's surface on the line as it's pulled toward the rod. As the line begins to drape over the caster's shoulder, execute a roll cast aimed at eye level. When the fly line straightens in front, move the rod forcefully to create a backcast. As the backcast straightens, perform a single haul and forward cast slowing the arm movement through the casting motion. The slow arm movement on the forward cast causes the loop to open and the heavier line and fly will land with a much softer splashdown. The half-roll, open loop cast lacks the aesthetic qualities of a tight-looped cast, but it delivers the fly efficiently while allowing the caster to eliminate the annoying and time-consuming strips of weighted line. The cast won't allow the pickup of 60-80 feet of line, of course, but with just a little practice it will enable line pickup of approximately 30 feet and with the single haul on the delivery 55 to 60 foot casts can be executed with relative ease. Best of all, the half-roll, open loop cast can be made while wading, seated in a float tube, canoe or any type of watercraft. The half-roll, open loop cast is often used to pick up floating line from the surface in fast water.

An important consideration when choosing sinking lines is the rate at which the line sinks. Most manufacturers indicate the sink rate on their sinking lines expressed in inches per second. This I.P.S. rating must be taken into account for the work you want the line to perform. We prefer full-sinking line rated at 6 I.P.S. for deeper sections of moving and still water if 7- or 8-weight rods are being used, but each fishing situation must be assessed independently. Another sink rate from an intermediate line that nearly creates neutral buoyancy to 5 I.P.S. may serve best in the water most frequently fished.

Another important consideration is the weight of the fly to be used in connection with sinking line. The expected function and structure content of the water body will dictate the possibilities. In heavy current, a heavily weighted fly may be necessary to keep the fly in bottom contact. Usually in these situations, the rate of current flow helps to prevent frequent hang-ups; roll casting past the rock eliminates the hang-up. In slower, but exceptionally rocky water it may be necessary to use a fast-sinking line with a fly of less weight. This arrangement allows the fly to remain out of harm's way while the weighted line snakes along the bottom as each strip causes the fly to bump into the substrate.

Finally, it's important to select the right leader to use in deep water. Water clarity must be considered. Clear, slow or still water means the fly is going to be scrutinized more carefully than if the water is fast, stained or both. Longer, finer leaders are the best choice in slow, clear situations. On the other hand, if the water is stained and the targeted rocks are so abundant as to dictate sinking line and a heavily weighted fly, the best choice is a short (3-1/2 to 6 feet) leader. This will prevent the unweighted fly from bowing toward the surface ineffectually.

It's hard to understate the importance of decisions made regarding terminal tackle. The choice of fly lines, leaders (length, suppleness), tippets (size, strength), and weight of the fly is a marriage that should be analyzed with care. Smallmouth bass can be downright arrogant in refusing a poorly presented fly. This lesson was indelibly imprinted in our memory by fishing a tiny step-across tributary of a favorite stream. The little spring-fed rivulet trickled off a mountain creating a stair-step of pools so clear that no mystery remained. The miniature bass could be plainly seen and darted for cover whenever a shadow crossed the water or a fly landed unnaturally. We watched rejection after rejection until the fly and its presentation were put together to the bass's satisfaction. On one visit to this peaceful trickle devoid of any other human sign, the fly had to flutter along in constant contact with the slab rock bottom — otherwise the 5-inchers would approach but never take our offering. The following morning that combination was summarily rejected until marabou-tailed flies were hopped along by raising and lowering the rod tip to create an undulating motion. Both days required 6X tippets and very sparsely tied flies. The days spent on that diminutive waterway are remembered every time our presentation becomes sloppy or our attention to detail lags as our hook-ups diminish.

The smallmouth's large-mouthed cousin is a glutton. It can often be taken on a fly that represents something other than prey that it is accustomed to feeding upon. "Old bucketmouth" will chase minnows into the shallows and cause them to spray into the air, yet interrupt its pursuit to grab a fly designed to look and act like a field mouse. First and foremost, the largemouth bass is an opportunist. Flies are most often chosen on the basis of their ability to suggest the bass's food in particular location, thus fly choice seems less critical. Smallmouth bass can be opportunistic feeders at times also, but, far more consistently, they are focused on a particular item on the menu and will reject flies that are suggestive of something else. If minnows are the dietary preference at the time, the angler had better show the smallmouth bass something that resembles a minnow. Sometimes this selectivity can be carried to an exacting level with rejections of everything except the right species, size, color, and action of their intended victims. Thankfully, these times are rare.

On one of our home lakes, this point was graphically driven home when we caught glimpses of smallmouths below our boat. We virtually emptied our fly boxes, changed lines to get different sink rates, and adjusted our tippet size and length numerous times without a single hit. Finally, we tied on something they wanted and enjoyed solid hits repeatedly before accidentally snagging one of the minnows that the smallmouths were attacking. It shouldn't have been a surprise that when the natural was laid beside the imitation the size was an exact match.

Our selection for bottom fishing is simple and basic, but we include several sizes of each prey represented. We match two bottom-hugging minnows, five nymphs, and, of course, crayfish.

Bottom Minnows

Sculpin are bottom dwelling minnows that live among the rocks in riffles or immediately downstream from a spring's well-oxygenated water. They have flat heads and usually a mottled brown appearance. It's essential to keep sculpin patterns near bottom. Our imitations are heavy and sinking lines help to keep their retrieves parallel to the bottom.

To work sculpins, we position ourselves above and to the side of the targeted riffle and make a down-and-across presentation while mending the line as necessary to keep the fly dead-drifting along the bottom. In faster riffles we impart short 3- to 4-inch strips at 3- to 5-second intervals. If the riffle is slower our strips will be made at progressively longer intervals. Our first casts are made to the nearest swift water of the riffle and the fly is fished along the initial seam, which is the first place where there are two different current speeds. By progressively lengthening each cast the entire riffle is thoroughly covered. After a few hits it will become clear which parts of the riffle are holding fish. If the stream is large it's best to concentrate on these areas and to keep moving. If the stream is smaller, more thorough coverage is possible.

Sculpin patterns are a staple in our stream fly boxes. Dave Whitlock created this one. We have used the pattern, along with numerous variations of our own, for years. As Dave said, "When smallmouth are holding deep and I suspect that they are feeding on bottom food forms such as sculpins, madtom catfish, darters, and crayfish I often go to this fly. And I'm often very glad I did."

Whitlock's Nearnuff Sculpin (Nearnuff Sculpin Olive)

Hook: TMC 5263, sizes 10, 8, 6, 4, barbless
Thread: Orange or olive Danville 6/0
Tail: 2 grizzly chicken body feathers or hen hackle (grizzly dyed golden brown or olive)
Body: Whitlock plus SLF dubbing #17 (sculpin olive) or #18 (sculpin golden brown)
Hackle: Grizzly dyed golden brown or olive neck or saddle hackle
Eyes: Wapsi dumbbell eyes (1/80, 1/60, 1/40 oz.)
Eye Paints: Yellow, red, and black Epoxy paint

Cements: Dave's Flexament, Zap-a-Gap
Note: Other pattern colors are tan or olive.

Stonecats and madtoms are primarily found in riffles and, as their names imply, are found in rocky streams and in wind-blown sections of rocky lakes. Their colors range from yellow/olive to blue/black with yellowish or cream colored undersides. Madtoms hide under rocks during the day, but emerge at night to feed. Despite that, we've enjoyed good success fishing their imitations in full sunlight as long as they are fished in contact with the bottom. The pattern we favor was shown to us by Arkansas smallmouth bass guide and nationally known artist Duane Hada.

Hada's Madtom

Hook: Mustad 3366 size
Eyes: Medium lead barbell eyes painted red with black pupils
Body: Cream Antron dubbing
Tail: Natural chinchilla zonker strip
Head: Cream two-tone wool, black on top. Trimmed to bullet shape.
Whiskers: Black Spandex

Nymphs On the Bottom

Hellgrammites are the larval stage of Dobsonflies. They can be the most abundant nymphs available to smallmouths even in areas where there seems to be few adults. Although there are heavy losses in their immature stages, they can grow to 3 inches or more in length. They are formidable-looking creatures, with large mandibles heavy enough to pinch an angler's finger. Hellgrammites are capable of propelling themselves through the water using an undulating swimming motion. This seductive action attracts smallmouths; consequently, raising and lowering the rod tip can present their imitations in a way that appears natural. Fly movements need to be subtle to keep them on the stream bottom where hellgrammites live under rocks and in crevices. An excellent pattern came from the creative mind of the late Texas tyer Michael Verduin.

Verduin's Hellgrammite

Hook: #4 stinger
Tail: Zonker strip 2 inches long
Body: Black Estaz
Hackle: Black Schlappen
Shellback: Swiss straw, black, 3 inches long
Mandibles: 10 mm black rubber ½-inch O-ring with about 90 degrees (a quarter) removed. Angle cuts for points.
Eyes: 4 mm bead chain, black
Note: Fly is tied hook point up.

Dragonfly nymphs usually occupy slower sections of streams or reside in lakes especially where the bottom is covered in silt. They are olive, tan, brown or gray in color, up to 2 inches long with rather stout bodies, and very aggressive feeders that propel themselves with quick, darting movements. The nymphs of some dragonfly species mature in a year; others species take as long as 5 years. They have flattened heads with large eyes and scoop-shaped mandibles capable of thrusting forward to capture prey. Their habit of being in constant motion to feed makes them continually available to feeding bass.

Michael Verduin's Dragonfly Nymph is a versatile imitation with very attractive action in the water. It is, in fact, a dragonfly nymph for the vertical drop that Michael also used for bluegills. It's a good pattern in tight places where there isn't enough slack water to work the fly before it's swept into the current. For fishing deep water, full-sinking line with a relatively short leader is required, but it can also be fished as a mid-depth fly using a short

Dobsonflies are the adult stage of the hellgrammite nymphs that smallmouths find irresistible.

strip-and-settle technique. Allow it to assimilate some water before casting to the targeted area.

Verduin's Dragonfly Nymph

Hook: Tiemco 200R size 6
Thread: Olive or tan 6/0
Eyes: Large black bead chain
Underbody: ¼ X ¼ X 5-inch piece of open cell foam
Body: Light olive vernille chenille and dark olive vernille chenille
Hackle: 1 strand olive Sili Legs cut in thirds
Wing: Olive zonker strip in dubbing loop, leather removed
Wing Case: Olive immature hen saddle hackle
Tying Instructions: Use an overhand-knot weave of vernille chenille to cover the foam underbody.

Damselfly nymphs are smaller and more slender than dragonfly nymphs but much more numerous. They are found around emergent vegetation or partially submerged brush and trees. They move with the same darting movements as dragonfly nymphs. The caster should take a position that enables the fly to be worked at various depths parallel to a weedbed, brush pile or tree limb. Darting strips of 3 to 4 inches interspersed with just enough of a pause to allow the fly to resettle to the desired depth is effective. Damselfly nymphs are not particularly effective when fished in open water or with a dead drift.

More than twenty seasons ago on a hot summer afternoon, we waded up an Ozarks stream to cast minnow imitations into a spring hole. After 2 hours of fruitless flailing, we decided to fish our way back to camp. As we entered a wide, slow pool edged in vegetation, we noticed several adult damselflies that seemed to be playing in the sunlight. Lacking flies that would match the adults, we knotted on nymphs and cast them beside the weeds. The response from the smallmouth population was immediate. We caught over a dozen bass of various sizes before the action slowed. That productive afternoon has kept us alert for summertime damselflies near emergent vegetation, and it's paid dividends on numerous occasions but never with the intensity of that original episode.

There are nearly 400 species of stoneflies in the United States and Canada alone. They come in a variety of sizes from ⅛ inch to at least 2 inches. Stonefly nymphs are available to bass year around, but many are most active in spring. An Ozark's Niangua River smallmouth enthusiast, Doug Farthing, ties our favorite Stonefly Nymph patterns.

Farthing's Mottled Stonefly Nymph

Hook: Mustad 9672 3XL size 8, bent to curve
Thread: Brown
Tail: Ginger goose biots
Abdomen: Golden pheasant tail fibers with copper wire rib, reverse wrapped
Thorax: Golden stone dubbing
Hackle: Ginger
Wing Case: Turkey tail

Another exceptionally effective pattern is one of Dave Whitlock's favorites, "Whitlock's Beadchain Sili-leg Red Fox Squirrel Nymph." We've had good success with it at the bases of river bluffs and rocky lake points. Dave advises, "This is the one fly that I have caught fish on everywhere in the world that I've traveled. It's my best nymph design and I think the beadhead/rubber legs pattern works so well with smallmouth because it resembles so many favorite smallmouth foods: crayfish, stonefly nymphs, large burrowing mayfly nymphs, and large caddis pupae." Here's how he ties it:

Whitlock's Beadchain Sili Leg
Red Fox Squirrel Nymph

Hook: TMC 5263, sizes 2, 4, 6, 8
Thread: Orange or black 6/0 Danville Waxed Flymaster
Weight: Gold bead and lead wire
Tail: Hair from red fox squirrel back
Rib: Gold oval tinsel
Abdomen: Whitlock plus SLF dubbing #2 (red fox squirrel nymph - abdomen)
Thorax: Whitlock plus SLF dubbing #1 (red fox squirrel nymph – thorax)
Legs: Dark ginger hen chicken back, pumpkinseed with green & orange flake Sili Legs Nymph
Head: Gold bead
Cement: Dave's Flexament

Impressionistic Action Flies

While the importance of smallmouth food replication cannot be overstated, there is unquestionable value to flies that don't specifically represent any bass food. Their action, depending on how they are presented and manipulated, is suggestive of several of the bass's dietary staples. The omnipresent Woolly Bugger, for example, might be taken as a minnow, leech, crayfish or nymph when it is stripped to produce a darting motion, steadily stripped, allowed to sink to the bottom or dead-drifted.

Recently, we've had consistent success with a modified version of one of our own patterns. In our book, *Largemouth Bass Fly-fishing: Beyond the Basics,* we described a fly we used on the vertical drop called Bass Bully. By substituting a rabbit strip for the tail and stacked and clipped wool for the head, the fly has acquired more uses. Whether it represents an escaping crayfish, foraging madtom, hellgrammite or wounded minnow we're not certain. It proved its value to us on an outing on North Arkansas'

Buffalo River, where a twenty-inch bronzeback fell for it in the first minutes of fishing, and it remains a "go to" fly for us. If you'd like to give the modified Bass Bully a try, here's how we tie it:

Wilson's Bass Bully (modified) (rust)

Hook: TMC 8089, size 10 wide gap
Thread: 3/0 rust
Weed Guard: (optional) 25-pound soft mono
Tail: Straight-cut rabbit strip the length of the hook shank
Body: Long Ice Chenille
Gills: medium red chenille
Collar: 2 full strips Metalflake Sili Legs, cut in half to make 4 pieces to form 8 legs
Eyes: extra small red barbell eyes with black pupils
Head: Sculpin wool, stacked and clipped
Note: The gills are a "ball" of red chenille formed by making two side-by-side wraps and adding a third wrap between the first two. The wraps should appear rounded like a small ball. The ball will help flare the legs and gives the fly a contrasting color that makes it more visible to the fish.

In addition to the rust pattern, we've been successful with olive, black, chartreuse, and a combination of gray and white. The fly can be fished along the edges of shoals and boulders, cast into the seams of converging currents, and fished as a true vertical drop fly in slow pools. Students in our warmwater fly-fishing school consistently caught more large fish on Bass Bully than other flies.

Another fly that represents any of several kinds of small-mouth prey is "Whitlock's Scorpion Fly" that utilizes a curly tail that provides a different action. Dave explains, "My Scorpion Fly provides a sort of 'grub & jig' lure for fly-fishers. It casts nicely, doesn't make a loud splash, sinks quickly, and swims or jigs with a real tantalizing action. It is also very snag-proof and relatively tangle free and can sometimes 'wake-up' those small-mouth when nothing else will."

Whitlock's Scorpion Fly

Hook: TMC 700, sizes 4, 1/0, barb bent down
Thread: Fluorescent orange Danville flat waxed nylon
Body Foundation and Double Dodger Snag Guard: Mason hard nylon (hook size 4 = .022", hook size 1/0 = .025")
Eyes: Gold Spirit River Real Eyes (size 4 = small, size 1/0 = medium)
Tails: Pumpkin/green-orange-black Wapsi Fly Tails (size 4 = small, size 1/0 = medium); brown grizzly marabou, rootbeer Krystal Flash
Body and Head: Brown and copper varigated tinsel chenille
Hackle Collar: Brown grizzly cock neck or saddle hackle (large and webby)
Legs: Pumpkin Sili Legs
Eye Paint: Black EZ Shape and pearl EZ Shape
Cements: Dave's Flexament, Zap-a-Gap
Note: Dave also ties his Scorpion in black pearl, rootbeer, white pearl, and chartreuse pearl colors.

Crayfish

In many watersheds the most important part of the small-mouth's diet is the crayfish. Fisheries biologists in some areas tell us that crayfish comprise up to 80% of the diet of smallmouths. The assumption by many is that the bass prefer them because they are a taste treat or that the crayfish are so high in calories that they grow and prosper from eating so many of them. While it's hard to determine what a fish tastes, it is known that an equal weight of minnow flesh far exceeds the caloric benefits of crayfish so it's likely that neither explanation is plausible. The truth of the matter is simply that crayfish are lousy swimmers and

Flies that closely imitate crayfish are favorites of most smallmouth fly fishers.

therefore easier to capture than most anything else. They are able to scull short distances by propelling themselves upward while undulating their tails, which causes them to move backwards. Current aids their escapes in streams but their attempts to flee are still not terribly effective. Crayfish survive, it would seem, by their sheer abundance.

Crayfish are freshwater crustaceans known by colloquial monikers such as crawfish, crawdad, and grass crab. Whatever you choose to call them, they are an important food item to virtually all freshwater gamefish and to none more important than smallmouth bass. There are numerous crayfish species that vary in size, coloring, and environmental preference. Some are found in swift rivers, some in sluggish rivers, and others only in stillwater. The lifespan of the crayfish is very short. Most males die at the end of their second year, while females last until their third summer. Fortunately, they are prolific reproducers.

Crayfish growth occurs when the hard shell is discarded and a new one is formed. This molting process may occur eight times or more during its first year of life. For a short period after the hard shell has been discarded the new shell is very soft and pliable. Their actual growth takes place during this soft-shell stage. This is when the molted crayfish, or "peeler" as it is known, is most desired by the smallmouth bass and other gamefish. Peelers are much lighter in coloration than they will be when the carapace hardens. They are light tan (some are even cream colored) and appear to be a bit transparent. We've heard some claims that smallmouths won't feed on those with hardened carapaces but that simply isn't so. The fish may prefer peelers because they are less menacing in their own defense, but we've caught lots of smallmouths on crayfish imitations that were dark shades of brown or olive and found regurgitated dark-colored naturals in the fishes' mouths as we landed them.

During the sunlit portion of the day crayfish hide under rocks and in the cracks of the substrate, but during periods of low light they move about to feed. This is when they are most available to gamefish and dictates to anglers when their imitations will be most successful. When summer's clear blue skies fade to darkness after sunset, crayfish and their smallmouth bass predators often become most active.

Most of the fly patterns designed to replicate crayfish emphasize the extended pincers because they are its most readily recognizable feature. Certainly, if the crayfish is simply crawling along the bottom the pincers will be extended away from its body, but if it's sculling away trying to escape, the pincers are held together nearly like human hands folded in prayer.

Patterns with extended pincers can be effective if the material used in their construction is pliable. If the material is heavy or stiff it will cause the fly to turn back and forth unnaturally as it is drawn through the water. It can even spin and turn the leader. In his excellent book, *Fly Fishing For Smallmouth Bass*, Harry Murray describes research done by the late Charlie

Brooks, whose underwater observations detected a "wobble" in flies tied with stiff pincers and subsequent bass refusals. Brooks recommended tying crayfish patterns "in the round," especially when moving water is involved. Our above-the-surface experience bears out the wobble factor.

In most stream situations, we fish crayfish patterns down-and-across while allowing the fly to dead-drift as the line is mended to facilitate depth. Slow strips are imparted occasionally and are accomplished by lifting and lowering to rod tip. It's important to keep crayfish flies in contact with the bottom. In stillwater or slower sections of streams a subtle silt trail may even enhance the presentation.

The Crayfish Hop

In sections of moving water where the current speed and water depth can be matched effectively with the weight of the fly, we use an upstream presentation called the "crayfish hop," first demonstrated to us by Minnesota guide and author Tim Holschlag. By casting floating line directly upstream, the weight of the fly promotes quick bottom contact. By lifting the rod tip, the phony crayfish is thrust upward into the current and is pushed along for a foot or more by the rushing water before diving back to the bottom as the rod tip is lowered. Strip only to remove slack line. Repeating the process until the fly must be picked up and recast allows the coverage of lots of water while simulating the movements of the escaping natural. Because there are so many variables, it's impossible to predetermine the relationship of water depth, current speed, leader length, and fly weight to complete the crayfish hop's execution. A little experimentation, however, will solve the puzzle. Annually, the crayfish hop produces some of our largest stream smallmouths. In stillwater we try to replicate the same action without the current by simultaneously lifting and stripping before lowering the rod tip. See Illustration 8-A.

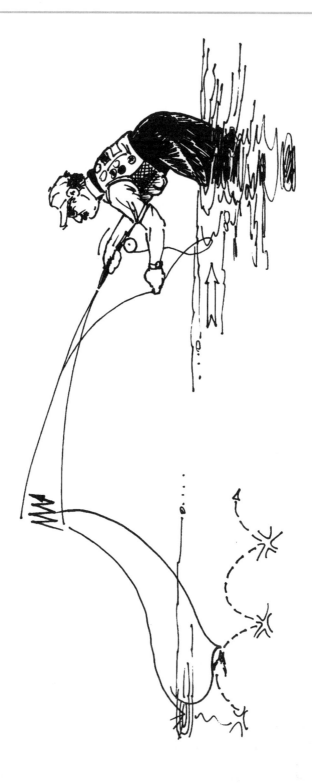

Illustration 8-A

Whenever we ask guides, tyers, and other fly-fishers to share their best smallmouth patterns, they invariably start talking about crayfish. Everyone seems to have a personal favorite. Here are nine crayfish recipes from impressionistic to realistic that we really like.

The late St. Louis-based demonstration fly tyer Doug Christian tied a pattern that fishes well. Here's his recipe:

Christian's Jig Crayfish

Hook: Eagle Claw 630, sizes 6 through 8
Weight: 1/32 oz. Lead jig head
Thread: Tan
Tail: Sparse deer hair
Antennae: Pheasant tail fibers
Rib: Copper wire
Overbody: ½-inch section of tan furry foam
Body: Tan furry foam; wrap 2 turns and attach the claws
Claws: 2 rabbit fur clumps
Hackle: Ginger
Tail: Excess furry foam from the Overbody

Christian's Jig Crayfish is effective when fished on the crayfish hop because of the fly's undulating motion.

Another effective pattern is tied by Arkansas guide Duane Hada.

Hada's Creek Crawler

Hook: Dai Riki 710, sizes 2 through 6
Thread: Brown
Mouth parts: Unstacked fox squirrel tail fiber and tuft of squirrel dubbing
Eyes: Melted mono
Body: Tan squirrel blend dubbing

Carapace: Clear plastic strip
Legs: Pheasant body feather
Weight: Barbell eyes, tied at hook eye
Head: Thread

Joe Schmuecker, of tying materials wholesaler Wapsi Fly, Inc. in Mountain Home, Arkansas, pioneered experimentation with cutting, dyeing, and tying pine squirrel strips. He modified a rabbit stripper to accommodate the smaller sizes needed for Canadian pine squirrel and ultimately developed two sizes, thin and regular. Use the thin strips for Schmuecker's Pine Craw.

Schmuecker's Pine Craw

Hook: TMC 8089, size 12
Antennae: Spanflex
Eyes: Medium brass barbell eyes painted brown
Claws: 2 strips of pine squirrel tied behind the eyes and tied to extend away from the hook shank.
Body: Pine squirrel wrapped to the hook eye

The subtle action of its fine fur makes the Pine Craw very effective, especially in pocket water. Natural colors work just fine, but the hide is compromised in the bleaching process so dyed colors, such as Joe's favorite, chartreuse, are difficult to get.

Steve Fritz, manager of the fly shop located in Bass Pro Shops Outdoor World in Branson, Missouri uses pine squirrel in his pattern as well. It's an excellent pattern that he's used successfully in the Boundary Waters Canoe Area north of Ely, Minnesota. It fishes equally well in more southerly climes. Here's Steve's pattern:

The Fritz Pine Craw

Hook: Mustad 79580 sizes 8 through 12
Thread: Brown Flymaster Plus

Weight: Micro or mini brass dumbbell eyes
Antennae: Black round rubber hackle, pearl or orange Krystal Flash, fox squirrel tail
Pincers: Brown pine squirrel strips twice the length of the hook shank
Body: Brown hare's mask dubbing mix
Carapace: Brown Ultra Suede
Legs: Pheasant rump feather
Paint: Waterproof marker for body, carapace, and pincers
Note: Other effective colors include olive and orange.

Louisiana fly tyer, Kyle Moppert swears by his modification of a Jack Garthside origination called The Rusty Sparrow. Here's Kyle's version:

The Rusty Sparrow (modified)

Hook: Mustad 9672, sizes 10 through 12
Thread: Flat waxed monocord, 6/0 brown
Weight: 1 to 3 amp lead wire to weight as desired
Tail: 2 medium reddish tipped marabou feathers from the butt side of a Ringneck Pheasant tail
Body: Squirrel dubbing mixed with Antron
Collar: Rusty-red Spey Hackle from the trailing edge of a Ring-neck Pheasant's rump
Collar: Aftershaft or filoplume feather found at the base of each full feather on the back of the Ringneck Pheasant

Kyle cautions that the aftershaft really soaks up head cement, and if the barbules take up the cement the fly loses all its action. He also recommends fishing the pattern "slower than slow."

One crayfish pattern has been a staple in smallmouth fly-fishers' boxes for many years. Dave Whitlock's Nearnuff Crayfish is durable and features plenty of natural action, which he points out, "is my favorite single most consistently productive, year-round smallmouth fly both for lakes and streams. It's also the fly that I get the most positive feedback on from other fly-fishers than any other I've designed for smallmouth, large sunfish, and carp."

Whitlock's Nearnuff Crayfish

Hook: TMC 5263, size 4, 6, 8, 10, barbless or barb bent down
Thread: Brown or orange Danville's Single Strand Floss
Eyes: 0.025" Mason hard monofilament painted with black lacquer
Antennae: Black nymph Sili Legs, pumpkin/green-orange barred Sili Legs, orange Krystal Flash
Nose: Natural dyed golden-brown rabbit hair
Body: (Thorax and Tail): Whitlock plus SLF dubbing #19 (crayfish natural-brown)
Pincers: Top: Grizzly dyed crayfish-brown hen neck or body feathers
Underside: Light tan hen neck or back feather
Legs: Grizzly dyed crayfish-brown webby saddle, neck or body feather
Tail Weight: Wapsi dumbbell eyes
Tail Paint: Crayfish-brown enamel undercoat, clear Epoxy overcoat
Tail Swimmers: Natural dyed golden-brown rabbit hair
Pincer and Sili Leg Antennae Tip Paint: Fluorescent red-orange acrylic enamel
Note: Other pattern colors are brown, gray or orange.

Terry Tanner, Bass Pro Shop's Outdoor World Fly-fishing Specialist, now retired, ties another crayfish pattern.

Tanner's Crawdad

Hook: Mustad 3366, size 8
Thread: Uni-thread 6/0
Tail Weight: Painted brass or lead eye
Pincers: Fox squirrel strips with hide on (Pine squirrel can be used for smaller sizes.)
Antennae: Paintbrush bristles or striped black hackles
Mouthparts: Pheasant tail fibers
Underbody: Wapsi's Crawdub
Eyes: Artificial flower stamens
Segmentation for abdomen: Copper wire
Carapace: Chamois or very thin leather

North Carolina smallmouth bass guide and tyer David Duffy ties a crayfish pattern that can take a pounding from the rocks or the bass. Here's Dave's recipe:

Crawman

Hook: Mustad 34007, #1/0 through 2
Thread: Olive
Body: Pearl/olive Estaz
Eyes: Barbell, tied at hook bend
Antennae: Peacock Krystal Flash, tied at hook bend
Claws: Olive rabbit fur clumps, tied on the sides near the hook bend
Head: Thread

Tackle representative David Halblom from Des Moines, Iowa uses rabbit strips to create a simple, but effective, crayfish pattern.

Halblom's Crayfish

Hook: TMC 200R size 6
Pincers: Light tan rabbit strips
Body: Rabbit strips wrapped around the hook shank
Ribbing: Fine copper wire
Eyes: Extra small nickel barbell

Please notice that the recipes given here represent many different sizes, colors, and weights. You may want to try these patterns for yourself or use some of the ideas we've presented to create your own.

In many bodies of water deep smallmouth-holding areas remain unexplored with flies. The keys to success include selecting the appropriate line, leader, and fly as well as keeping the line and fly under control. Stay alert for the slightest hesitation or twitch in the fly line and set the hook vigorously in deep water. Unlocking the secrets of deep-water fly-fishing will likely increase both the numbers and sizes of your catch.

CHAPTER 9
FOR THE LOVE OF SMALLMOUTHS

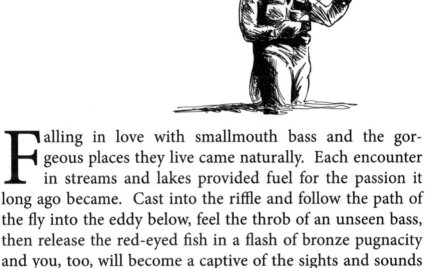

Falling in love with smallmouth bass and the gorgeous places they live came naturally. Each encounter in streams and lakes provided fuel for the passion it long ago became. Cast into the riffle and follow the path of the fly into the eddy below, feel the throb of an unseen bass, then release the red-eyed fish in a flash of bronze pugnacity and you, too, will become a captive of the sights and sounds that accompany the pursuit of this impressive species. Those of us who share the love of smallmouth fishing must agree to work tirelessly to preserve it and even to improve the quality of our sport.

Too many anglers believe that restocking is the final solution to improving the quality and quantity of the fisherman's catch. Unfortunately it isn't nearly that simple. While stocking has unquestionably extended the smallmouth's original range, restocking might pose a dramatic threat when diminished native populations are supplemented with hatchery-reared fish. The interbreeding of native smallmouth bass, fish that evolved in and have adapted to their particular waters through natural selection, with the introduced population results in offspring that may be less able to survive the physiological stress of their environments. The results of restocking are irreversible. In addition to the understandable hesitation some fisheries biologists express in confronting the ethical question of altering the uniqueness of native fish populations, restocking native populations also runs the risk of introducing fish diseases into the water system.

Many anglers believe that quality smallmouth fishing can be created simply through state regulations that restrict creel limits by size and/or quantity, as though releasing fish alone will improve the fishery. Catch-and-release certainly helps support smallmouth populations in waters that receive lots of angling attention, but releasing captured smallmouths is only part of the

Grazing cattle on riverbanks results in pollution and degradation of smallmouth bass habitat.

undertaking to preserve our resources. Stocking and regulations will not support smallmouth bass if there are no suitable places for them to live and reproduce.

Over decades of writing about warmwater fly-fishing we have witnessed a staggering lack of appreciation for the resources anglers have in their own backyards. In many states across the nation, smallmouth bass are disappearing from their streams and lakes at an alarming rate. Unfortunately, there are many threats to our native smallmouth bass. Most often it's not just one problem alone that reduces the sizes and numbers of smallmouth bass, but several problems together. Each by itself is dangerous to the fish population, and consequently to our sport, but when combined the problems can be deadly. Not all of the threats discussed here are found throughout the smallmouth's range, yet no region is immune. Clearly, we must come to understand that habitat determines the quality of smallmouth fishing.

Streambank Degradation

As anglers, we are concerned about the living things that occupy the streams we fish. Many streams that were excellent smallmouth bass fisheries have succumbed to subdivisions, shopping malls, parking lots, and new roads that have been added to the landscape. Farmers sometimes plow fields right to the water's edge; many graze their herds on riverbanks and use streams as water sources for cattle. Other landowners have bulldozed streambanks to create beaches for recreation and removed trees in riparian corridors to afford better views of the streams. The aquatic food chain is dependent upon streambank vegetation. Trees, brush, and weeds on streambanks are essential to smallmouth habitat. In addition to shading the water to prevent warming, tree roots hold the banks and reduce the amount of soil and gravel that rains wash into the stream. Stream bank degradation loosens the substrate that is vital to the invertebrates smallmouth feed upon and sends it downstream with subsequent rainfalls. The effects of stream bank degradation aren't always immediately evident, but in time the effects of an accumulation of abuses can devastate once-healthy streams. The knowledge and technology to alleviate the problem of streambank degradation is readily available. Building catch basins that reduce erosion and planting trees, bushes, and grass to help stabilize the stream bank, for example, can significantly reduce the degradation.

Our European heritage led us to adopt the attitude that land ownership meant we could do anything we wished with or to the land. In the 21st century it seems obvious that our notion of land ownership must change. At best our ownership lasts only a short time. We must come to view the time as our period of stewardship. Poor land-use practices are shortsighted and counterproductive to the long-range goals of landowners and their heirs, as well as other river users. Unless we can educate our younger citizens about less destructive land ownership and teach them to be sensitive to the health of our waterways, stream bank degradation will continue for generations to come.

Pollution

Most recognize that piles of dead fish on a lake shore or stream bank from a deadly toxic spill is an ecological disaster. Although such incidents gain publicity that graphically illustrates the harm that has been done, few take notice of the many cases of creeping ground source pollution from the septic tanks of bankside homes that leeches into lakes and streams. The runoff from pastures, croplands, and subdivisions that have been treated with pesticides, herbicides, and fertilizers; and runoff of storm water from nearby villages, is non-point pollution that alters the chemistry of the water and is equally, if less spectacularly, destructive. Point-source pollution often comes from inadequate sewage treatment, waste treatment plant effluents that are accidentally flushed into rivers, and waste from livestock that is deposited directly into streams or lakes. Fixing pollution problems ranges from the simple and relatively inexpensive, as is the case in fencing livestock out of rivers and providing an alternative water source, to complex projects, such as modern sewage treatment plants that might cost millions of dollars.

Smallmouth bass are sensitive to lower pH levels, and it is one of the first fish species to be affected by acid rain. In the northern portion of the smallmouth's range, acid rain, which is the result of air pollution from industrial operations and the burning of fossil fuels, has altered the chemical makeup of some lakes and streams to the extent that their waters are now devoid of smallmouths altogether. In other waters, acid rain has inhibited fish reproduction and growth.

Channelization

In locations where row crop agriculture is a major component of the economy, some streams that historically had supported smallmouth populations have been straightened, or channelized, to speed runoff from heavy rains so that fields will not be inundated long enough to destroy crops. Adjacent fields have been tiled, in many cases, to further expedite the runoff. Streams below channelized sections are adversely affected by silt, debris, and flooding. The remains of once pristine native smallmouth bass fisheries have become nothing more than heavily silted, polluted ditches that are hard-pressed to harbor anything but bullheads. Streams that have been lost through channelization are permanently lost, but future projects need to be carefully scrutinized.

Gravel Mining

Where the size of rocks in streambeds and flood plains meets human needs for use as gravel, the practice of hauling gravel from streambeds is as old as homesteading in the region. In some cases landowners have mined the rock for their own use while

Bulldozing streambeds and gravel mining have resulted in the loss of countless miles of smallmouth bass habitat.

others have created commercial enterprises based on the natural abundance. Some even believe that the stream will lose its fish population if the gravel isn't removed to make deeper holes for the fish. The result of removing or relocating the gravel is loosened rocks that are easily washed into deeper holes below when the stream swells after rains. When the holes fill, the displaced volume of water is forced to rearrange even more of the streambed. Eventually the waterway becomes wider with a network of shallow channels. The shallow water warms intolerably for smallmouth bass, offers no cover and little or no food, oxygen is depleted, and without a riffle-pool-riffle arrangement the stream no longer meets their needs. Some move to another section of river, which already has a population of fish that equals the carrying capacity of the section. As the available food becomes depleted, the population stunts and spawning success diminishes. If the mined gravel is washed on site, the effluent from the process enters the stream as warm, turbid water that adversely affects aquatic life in the stream. In addition, landowners or operators do not restore some gravel mining areas when the site is abandoned and the result is lost real estate when the streambanks are further eroded after rains. Gravel mines wreck the river's recreational potential, drastically reduce its dependent wildlife, and destroy its aesthetics.

Dams

Dams on free-flowing streams have destroyed many miles of gamefish habitat. Although the smallmouths can find new areas in which to live in impounded waters, dramatic fluctuations in water levels interfere with spawning and reduce food resources. Dams block spawning routes within streams and dramatically reduce stream flow, which allows silt to cover nesting areas and clouds the water. In some cases, dams trap the stream's smallmouths so that they become isolated from the genetic diversity that strengthens their population. Smallmouths are often forced to compete with largemouth bass and other gamefish for forage and cover. Populations dwindle as they are relegated to a few areas within the impoundment. The waters downstream of the dam become smaller and shallower due to the drastic reduction of the stream's flow, which results in less water that smallmouths can inhabit. The removal of dams that are no longer needed is important to the restoration of smallmouth streams because it improves water quality, which allows more diverse invertebrates to thrive and become food for smallmouths. Dam removal alone, however, doesn't repair the damage to the stream's habitat that occurred over time.

Low-water road crossings on small streams that don't allow

water to flow underneath or over them except during floods have some of the same detrimental effects as dams. Smallmouth bass and other fish, including the baitfishes that bass depend upon to survive, are unable to move upstream and down to spawn or find suitable cover during the extremes of summer and winter. The stream's flow is interrupted, which results in more silt, fewer invertebrates, and reduced water quality.

Spotted Bass

Some watersheds that are traditional smallmouth waters have been stocked with Kentucky Spotted Bass. The "spots" have reproduced well and provide additional catchable fish, but smallmouth devotees point to a decline in their favorite species and thus blame the spots for supplanting bronzebacks. Some fisheries biologists have told us that there's no evidence that smallmouths are being replaced and that it's more likely that the "spots" have simply moved into waters smallmouths weren't using. Even if that assertion is true, there's no question that the two species compete for the same food. If crayfish suffered a decline, even in some areas, the smallmouth population would be adversely affected. Other fisheries biologists express concerns about the spotted bass's encroachment and the resulting decline in smallmouth numbers. In some areas, minimum length limits for spotted bass have been decreased and creel limits increased in the hope that angling can help reverse the trend.

If there is any replacement of smallmouths by spotted bass it's a poor trade off for sportsmen. Stream spots rarely reach the maximum size of smallmouths and, at least in the opinion of fanciers of bronzebacks, spots lack some of the latter's fighting spirit. Further, the two species frequently interbreed, which creates hybrids that are generally smaller and corrupt the smallmouths' genetic integrity.

What You Can Do

The multiplicity of serious threats facing our smallmouth populations is daunting to even the staunchest advocate. Decades of unwise decisions and abuse have brought about the general decline in the quality of watersheds that propagate smallmouths, and since the negative changes mostly occur in a slowly unfolding progression the loss seems inevitable. If we don't own the land along the streams and possess no base of political support, we feel powerless. The attitude of those who accept their helplessness is nearly as detrimental as those who over-harvest, pollute, in-stream gravel mine, etc. Both positions are incompatible with good smallmouth fishing. All of us who fish for this great species have a responsibility to protect it.

Perhaps the place to initiate the execution of our responsibility is to examine our own code of ethics as fly-fishers. First, we have a responsibility to practice our sport within the law. Our licenses, tags, and stamps pay for enforcement of regulations and enhancement projects that benefit our sport. We should be concerned with catch-and-release, of course, but also with the quality of the release. Make certain the fish we are releasing is recovered. Holding the fish gently in an upright position while pointing it upstream facilitates the fish's safe recovery. Barbless hooks are an option worthy of consideration because they have only to be backed out rather than twisted and pulled from the bass's flesh. This is particularly helpful in the safe release of deeply hooked fish. Deeply taken flies should be sacrificed by being cut off; the hook will be an annoyance to the fish for a day or two, but there is a far greater chance of the fish's survival if the line is cut. The acid on our hands burns the protective slime off the fish we are trying to release, which makes the fish susceptible to parasites and diseases so that their ultimate survival is threatened. Be sure to wet your hands before making contact with the fish to dilute the acid and reduce the potential harm to the fish. By handling the captured fish as little as possible the risk of injury is also reduced. The best release is gentle, quick, and performed beneath the water's surface.

Our ethics must also engage the environment in which small-mouths live. We need to do our part in providing clean water-ways. It takes very little effort to carry out the refuse we encounter while fishing. Cans, bottles, and wrappers thoughtlessly left behind by others can be removed by putting them into a small bag carried along in your watercraft or attached to your belt if you're wading. It's important that we pass along all our positive conservation ethics to the next generation. Their perception of fly-fishing for smallmouth bass and their concern for the fishery will only be positive if we guide them through words and ex-amples toward becoming the kind of sportsmen with whom we want to share our secret fishing places. If we fail to lead the next generation toward becoming positive stewards of the streams and lakes the time might come when fly-fishing for smallmouth bass in their native waters is a distant memory. How sad it would be for our children and our grandchildren to be unable to enjoy the benefits we've all derived from this grand pursuit.

While there are many threats to the smallmouth's well be-ing, there are lots of positive steps already being taken. Many states have organized water quality monitoring programs that are staffed at the local level by volunteers. By testing their waters and keeping records, they are able to alert the appropriate state departments of natural resources and conservation of changes in streams and lakes that might affect wildlife and fisheries. Al-though some training is required, scout troops, school science classes, retirees, and fishing clubs are among the participants. The number of people who generously give their time and ef-fort to help protect our water resources is testimony to the na-tion's grass roots concern about clean water. The resurgence of interest in fishing for smallmouth bass in the past decade has also created a network of people willing to help protect them. There have been significant strides made to recapture lost ar-eas of smallmouth habitat with improvements to water quality.

The best release is gentle, quick and performed beneath the surface.

Downstream sections of streams too warm to sustain trout, especially in the northeastern United States, have seen revitalized bronzeback populations.

As anglers our strongest voices and most important contributions are created when we work together. There are many proactive groups that have accomplished quite a lot with regard to educating the public, purchasing land for preservation and public access, rehabilitating habitat, cleaning up streams and lakes, promoting trophy smallmouth regulations and catch-and-release waters, lobbying legislators to protect habitat, and much more.

The Federation of Flyfishers and The Smallmouth Alliance are two organizations that are directly involved in preserving and restoring smallmouth bass habitat. Preservation and restoration of free-flowing streams has several supportive organizations, such as Nature Conservancy and American Rivers. By practicing good fishing and conservation ethics, joining organizations that promote the same, and passing our knowledge, skills, and enjoyment on to the next generation, we ensure that tomorrow's smallmouth fishing adventures will be even more productive and enjoyable than those we've already experienced.

BIBLIOGRAPHY

Bauer, Erwin A. *The Bass Fishermen's Bible*. Garden City, NY: Doubleday & Company, Inc. 1961

Bunt, Christopher M., Steven J. Cooke, and David P. Philipp. "Mobility of Riverine Smallmouth Bass Related to Tournament Displacement and Seasonal Movements." Black Bass: Ecology, Conservation, and Management. David P. Philipp and Mark S. Ridgway, eds. Bethesda, Maryland: American Fisheries Society, 2002

Henshall, James Alexander. *Book of The Black Bass*. Cincinnati, Ohio: R. Clarke & Co. 1881

Holschlag, Tim. *Stream Smallmouth Fishing*. Harrisburg, Pennsylvania: Stackpole Books, 1990

Kreh, Lefty. *Fly Fishing For Bass: Smallmouth, Largemouth and Exotics*. Birmingham, Alabama: Odysseus Editions, Inc. 1993

Lucas, Jason. *Lucas on Bass Fishing*. New York: Dodd, Mead & Co., Inc. 1962

Lyons, John and Paul Kanehl. "Seasonal Movements of Smallmouth Bass in Streams." Black Bass: Ecology, Conservation, and Management. David P. Philipp and Marks S. Ridgway, eds. Bethesda, Maryland: American Fisheries Society, 2002

McClane, A. J., ed. *McClane's Standard Fishing Encyclopedia*. Holt, Rinehart, and Winston. 1965

Morris, Skip. *The Art of Tying the Bass Fly*. Portland, OR: Frank Amato Publication, Inc. 1996.

Murray, Harry. *Flyfishing For Smallmouth Bass*. New York: The Lyons Press, 1989

Nemes, Sylvester. *The Soft-Hackled Fly*. Old Greenwich, Connecticut: Chatham Press, 1975.

Pflieger, William L. *The Fishes of Missouri*, Revised Edition. Jefferson City, Missouri: Missouri Department of Conservation, 1997.

Pflieger, William L. *The Crayfishes of Missouri*. Jefferson City, Missouri: Missouri Department of Conservaiton, 1996.

Philipp, David P. and Julie E. Claussen. "Loss of Genetic Diversity Among Managed Populations." Illinois Natural History Survey. U.S. Geological Survey Website: http://biology.usgs.gov/s+t/noframe/e221.htm

Reynolds, Barry and John Berryman. *Beyond Trout: A Flyfishing Guide*. Boulder, Colorado: Johnson Publishing Company. 1995

Ryan, Will. *Smallmouth Strategies for the Flyrod*. New York: The Lyons Press, 1996

Springer, Craig. "FFF's Conservation Watch," *The Flyfisher*. Milwaukee, Oregon: Frank Amato Publications, Inc., Summer 2001

Stewart, Dick and Farrow Allen. *Flies For Bass and Panfish*. Intervale, New Hampshire: Northland Press, 1992

Sosin, Mark and Bill Dance. *Practical Black Bass Fishing*. New York: Crown Publishers, Inc. 1974

Sura, Dan, and Dave Csanda, Bob Ripley, Ron and Al Lindner, Doug Stange, Larry Dahlberg. *Smallmouth Bass: An In-Fisherman Handbook of Strategies.* Brainerd, MN: In-Fisherman Inc., 1984.

Waterman, Charles F. *Black Bass & the Fly Rod.* Harrisburg, Pennsylvania: Stackpole Books. 1993

Wilde, Gene R. "Dispersal of Tournament-caught Black Bass." Fisheries Management & Ecology. Volume 28 Number 7. Blackwell Publishing: Malden, Massachusetts. 2003

Index

V

W